# What People Are Saying About
# Men Chase, Women Choose

"*Men Chase, Women Choose* is unreal! We've always known that *The Rules* work, now we know why! Filled with statistics, anecdotes and humor, Dawn Maslar's new book *Men Chase, Women Choose* explains the science behind why women need to play hard to get!! A must-read for single women!"

—**Ellen Fein** and **Sherrie Schneider**, coauthors of *All The Rules* and *Not Your Mother's Rules*

"Finally, a book that doesn't treat finding true love like a Nora Ephron movie! Biology, nature, evolution... they all play a role in helping us find that special someone. Or in keeping them from us forever. And in *Men Chase, Women Choose* you'll understand, once and for all, the difference between a love that endures, and a lust that flames out once the lights come on. Anyone who still thinks making poor decisions, falling for 'bad boys,' or not having the right looks, money, career, car, or hair is the reason you can't meet the person of your dreams, Dawn Maslar has your wake-up call."

—**Eric Rogell**, author of *The Art of War for Dating*

"Dawn Maslar is Barbara DeAngelis meets Bruce Lipton."

—**Ernest Chu**, author of *Soul Currency*

"I love *Love*. I believe that deep down, we all do. But many people are reluctant to *own* their love of love. It's fear that keeps them distanced from their oh-so-human longings for genuine connection. Fear of rejection. Fear of hurt. Fear of disclosure. Thankfully, Dawn Maslar shines the light of cutting-edge scientific information onto these fears, proving once and for all that love is our evolutionary destiny.

Understanding the anthropological principles that underlie our responses to love does not lessen its beauty and enigmatic wonder, but allows us to clearly view love as a biological responsibility. Dawn Maslar is undoubtedly making the world a better place by sharing her wisdom in this funny, smart, and provocative guide."

—**Lisa McCourt**, author
of *Juicy Joy: 7 Simple Steps to Your Glorious, Gutsy Self*

"*Men Chase, Women Choose* is warm and witty with a perfect balance of science and insight. You'll find yourself wondering why a book of this magnitude didn't come out sooner. But like everything else in life, all in due time."

—**Gabe Berman**, author
of *Live Like a Fruit Fly*

"Dawn Maslar's book *Men Chase, Women Choose* offers many insightful ideas on sex and relationships. Whether in between relationships or currently in one, readers will find valuable insight on how men and women interact with each other and what dynamics long-term relationships need to work. Maslar mixes scientific concepts, often with humor, making it a light and enjoyable read. I highly recommend this book to anyone searching to find true love."

—**Theresa Braun**, author
*Groom and Doom: A Greek Love Story* and a dating blogger

"Such a great guidebook to dating! I really appreciated the current information about creating a dating profile and the science behind love. A must-read for anyone!"

—**Jenette F.**

# MEN CHASE, WOMEN CHOOSE

## The Neuroscience of Meeting, Dating, Losing Your Mind, and Finding True Love

### DAWN MASLAR, MS

Health Communications, Inc.
Deerfield Beach, Florida

*www.hcibooks.com*

Library of Congress Cataloging-in-Publication Data
is available through the Library of Congress

© 2016 Dawn Maslar, MS

ISBN-13: 978-07573-1925-9 (Paperback)
ISBN-10: 07573-1925-4 (Paperback)
ISBN-13: 978-07573-1926-6 (ePub)
ISBN-10: 07573-1926-2 (ePub)

Publisher: Health Communications, Inc.
          3201 S.W. 15th Street
          Deerfield Beach, FL 33442–8190

*Cover photo by Rafael A. Acosta*
*Cover design by Larissa Hise Henoch*
*Interior design and formatting by Lawna Patterson Oldfield*

# CONTENTS

Introduction ♥ 1

Chapter 1: Love Is All in Your Head ♥ 3
Chapter 2: Men Chase, Women Choose ♥ 25

## Part I: MEETING
Chapter 3: Attraction ♥ 45
Chapter 4: The Art and Science of Attraction ♥ 75

## Part II: DATING
Chapter 5: Love Potion ♥ 89
Chapter 6: Dating Wisdom: What Works, What Doesn't ♥ 113

## Part III: LOSING YOUR MIND
Chapter 7: Falling in Love ♥ 155

## Part IV: **FINDING LOVE**

Chapter 8: Real Love　♥　185

Chapter 9: The Truth About Happily Ever After　♥　209

Conclusion　♥　233

Endnotes　♥　235

# INTRODUCTION

"What am I doing wrong?"

I looked up to see a beautiful blond woman with familiar green eyes. Her voice cracked as she held back her tears. "I thought I did everything right, but here I am again," she said.

Her name was Jessica, and we'd originally met when she came to me for relationship coaching two years earlier. She had a frustrating and almost predictable relationship pattern. She would meet an amazing man, and the relationship would start out with wonderful promise. But when she dated, she would get crazy. Her anxiety level would increase and she would either jump into a sexual relationship where she fell in love but he didn't, or she would pull away, finding some flaw or perceived mistrust in him. The details of each relationship were different, but eventually a glaring problem would arise. She told me the first man had lied, the second worked too much, and the third chatted with women online. Now she was here again, looking for help.

I had worked with her in the past to break her pattern of picking men that were wrong for her, but now another problem had arisen. She was picking better men, but she still couldn't seem to find love.

Her problem this time wasn't with men but with herself and the dating process.

Love isn't just one thing that you luckily fall into. Finding and maintaining lifelong love is a process with several stages that are biologically different from one another. Because the stages are different, you can feel different emotions during each phase. Most people, particularly women, have trouble with anxiety. As you move along the path to lifelong love, your level of anxiety fluctuates, sometimes to the point of panic. At other times, your anxiety is gone, and you feel euphoric. This euphoric phase is the one that most people associate with love.

My goal in writing this book is to explain what happens on the path to lifelong love. I'll point out the twists and turns as well as the potholes, the places that can cause trouble and hurt you. When you understand the science of love, it will help you easily and effortlessly find nourishing and passionate, long-lasting love.

# CHAPTER

# LOVE IS ALL
# IN YOUR HEAD

You know the feeling. You can't wait for the day to end so you can be together. You look at the picture of you two and your heart fills with joy as a big smile spreads across your face. You feel so light you almost glide, with just your toes barely glancing the floor. You feel giddy, even euphoric. At any moment small woodland creatures are going to hop out to greet you. Birds will twirl around your head. Any minute now Pharrell Williams is going to walk out singing *Happy* as you dance with the animals. *Clap along if you feel like happiness is the truth.* It's a magical, special time. You know you have hit the jackpot of life—you have fallen in love.

This is the feeling everyone is looking for, that sensation that you're special to someone else, that you've found that other person, that "better half," your soul mate, to experience life with. You have a partner and a friend who loves you with every fiber of their being, and you feel the same way about them. You wonder how you could've ever lived without them. You are loved!

A study from the University of Iowa confirms this universal search for love. When researchers looked at the number one thing men and woman wanted in their lives, they discovered it was exactly the same for both—mutual attraction and love.[1] Love is what this book is about. I'll explain where love comes from, how to find it, how long each phase is (yes, there are phases), and how you can make love last. In these pages, I explain the biological processes that create that sensation of being in love. I'll show you what steps are needed to reach it and how those steps are different for men than for women. I'll explain why dating can be so nerve-wracking. You naturally desire love, but getting love requires you to be vulnerable. You have an innate fear of being vulnerable. The process of becoming vulnerable goes against your other natural desire for self-preservation.

One of the biggest fears is that you'll fall in love and become vulnerable while the other person won't. The pain of unrequited love for some people can be so great that they give up looking for love altogether. But you don't have to. When you understand how love works, you will be able to make educated decisions that make finding and keeping it almost effortless.

Did you know that love is a chemical reaction that affects your brain? That falling in love is only one phase of a multiphase process? That falling in love changes the way your brain functions? That the actions you take at the beginning of a relationship can either cause the other person to leave or to fall in love with you? That the feeling of "falling in love" lasts for a predictable amount of time? That "falling in love" and "being in love" are very different things? Not only that, but you don't have control of the neurological changes associated with *falling* in love, but you do have control of *being* in love. But the most important thing to know is that love is a biological process, and once you understand the science behind the way love works, it makes finding and keeping love easy.

Over the course of this book, I will walk you through the different brain states of love and their biochemical and physiological differences, and how those differences make you feel at each stage. I'll explain what you can do if you want love in your life, whether new love, to keep a love you've found, or to rekindle the spark that you two once had. Understanding the science of love gives you the power to make informed decisions about the most important choice you'll ever make—to love.

I'm Dawn Maslar, and I'm known as the "Love Biologist." Before I share what I've learned while researching the science of love, maybe I should explain how this all started.

It was an accident—a real, screeching-tires type of accident.

I had recently relocated to southern Florida after a divorce, and my life finally felt like it was coming back together in a better way. I had just landed a coveted, full-time temporary biology professorship at Broward Community College, in warm, sunny, subtropical Davie, Florida.

Only a month before, I had purchased a Yamaha V Star 850 motorcycle. The 850 was fast enough to get me around but not so heavy that it would knock me over if I tried to walk it. A motorcycle is not the most practical or safest form of transportation, especially in a heavily populated area. But when I rode the bike, I felt an exciting sense of freedom. Even more important than the exhilaration of the ride, it provided me with a means to get closer to my bad-boy biker crush.

That's right, I was a thirty-something divorced woman with several degrees and a big, fat, teenage-like crush on a biker. He was rugged and unconventional, with long, braided hair. He worked with his hands; they were gnarled, callused, and damn sexy. He had tattoos on his arms, and he walked with a mesmerizing, sexy swagger that said, "Come and get me, Dawn—if you dare." I wanted him, but I didn't know how to get his attention. I knew I was going to have to work hard to get it. With that belief, I slowly began interjecting myself into his world; I would try to strike up a conversation with him whenever I could. I also started writing down my thoughts about him. I ended up turning one of those into an article about my attraction to a bad-boy biker, and was then offered a column in a local biker magazine. It seemed that I wasn't the only woman out there with this type of fascination.

One fateful day, a balmy breeze gently swayed the palm fronds as I biked up the long, tree-lined drive bordered on each side by tranquil ponds, and joined the rest of the campus traffic. At the top of the road was an intersection with a parking lot. I saw the late-model, silver, four-door sedan waiting to cross the road. Motorcycle schools warn you that intersections are the most dangerous spots for motorcyclists (where the majority of motorcycle fatalities occur). Therefore, you're advised to make eye contact with the driver whenever possible.

As I approached the intersection, I looked at the driver. We made eye contact. I knew she saw me, and that I had the right-of-way— even though a right-of-way is an absurd concept for a biker (like an ant thinking he has the right-of-way when he meets a shoe).

As I entered the intersection, I saw a flash of silver out of the corner of my eye. The driver had pulled out, and I was going to hit her. This is one of the worst types of accidents for a motorcyclist. If she hit the side of me, I would go down, maybe break a leg or an arm, but if I hit the side of her car, I would most likely be launched over the hood. This is the nastiest type of accident because you often land on your head. The outcome might be a broken neck, brain damage, or death.

The next thing I remember is watching my motorcycle skid sideways through the intersection without me. I should've heard noise, but it was as if I were listening underwater. In dreamlike slow motion, I looked down and saw that I was standing in the middle of the intersection. A silver fender was just an inch from my thigh. There was no blood. I turned and looked at the driver. She looked back at me, her face twisted in terror, and then looked away. Someone ran up from behind me.

"Are you okay?" he asked.

Two more guys ran up, picked up my motorcycle, and walked it off to the side of the road.

I felt my legs, then my head. I was still wearing my helmet. I was fine. I walked over to my bike. It had a few scratches on the handlebar grips, but it looked intact.

"Should I call the police or campus security?" the man asked.

"No, I'm okay. I just need to get to my office," I said.

He waved. When I turned back, the silver car was gone.

I tried to jump right back on the bike, but my legs began to shake violently. Somehow I managed to maneuver the bike into a parking spot and scurried to my office. I was scared and needed comfort. I decided to call *him*.

In my mind, this was the perfect scenario. I fantasized about what would happen next. I would call Dirk (not his real name, but it should've been) and it would play out like this:

"I was in an accident," I would say.

"Oh my God, are you all right?" he would ask.

"Yes, but I'm shaking like a leaf. I'm not sure I can ride my bike back home," I would say.

"Oh no, don't worry about that. I'll come and ride your bike home for you. Then we can grab some dinner," he would say.

He would don his Superman cape, swoop down, and rescue me. He would take me home and hold me with my face buried in his muscular chest. I would breathe in his musky scent until my fears subsided. Then he would guide my chin to bring my lips close to his. Our kiss would melt into an evening of enchanted lovemaking. Oh, this was going to be good.

It was time to turn this fantasy into reality, so I dialed his number.

"Yeah."

"Dirk?"

"Yes."

"It's Dawn; how are you?

"I'm fine, but . . ." he paused.

"What's wrong?" I asked.

"I really can't talk to you."

*What? Wait, this was not how it was supposed to go.*

"Is this a bad time?" I asked.

"Well, no. I really can't talk to you anymore," he said.

"Anymore?"

"Yes, I need to stop talking to you."

"Why?" I whined like a two-year-old.

"I met someone, and I asked her to marry me."

I was stunned. I looked at the phone, which had fallen, along with my hand, onto the desk. Whether the cause was the accident or his words—most likely a combination of both—I was in shock. How could he marry someone else? What was I doing wrong?

~○

This painful experience, and the realization that resulted from it, changed my life. I embarked on a type of healing that helped me break my addiction to men who couldn't love me. I was so enamored by the process that I wrote a book about it titled *The Broken Picker Fixer*. It was instantly successful. Overnight, I had a radio show and an advice column on a popular website. I sold the rights to the book and it was republished under the title *From Heartbreak to Heart's Desire: Developing a Healthy GPS (Guy Picking System)*. The next thing I knew, my weeks were filled with writing, workshops, and coaching calls. I loved it, but at the end of the day, I still had that nagging question . . . How? I now knew how *not* to pick the wrong men, but I really wanted to know how to find lasting love with the right man.

I wanted to understand what it takes to find enduring love. I wanted a best friend and a lover. I wanted someone who I could travel this life with, a trusted, loving partner. I wanted to be one part of the little old couple sitting on the park bench, holding hands and reminiscing about our wonderful life together. I wanted to know how to get there.

I began by spending hours in the self-help/relationship section of the bookstore, but I walked away consistently unsatisfied with opinions and rules. Most of the advice was empirical and based on the author's beliefs or personal experience. I wanted more. I wanted facts derived from hard science. If there were biological principles surrounding love and dating, I wanted to understand them. I wanted to be able to apply them to any situation. I wanted to understand the way love works so I could follow that path all the way to that park bench. And, I'm glad to tell you, that's what this book does.

## HOW DOES LOVE WORK?

I've heard this question more times than I can count in workshops, coaching sessions, and presentations, and it's the question I set out to answer after my divorce and the subsequent relationships that seemed promising but went nowhere. During the many years I spent looking for the answer, I riffled through hundreds of stacks of dusty library journals and researched sources as diverse as *Psychoneuroendocrinology* and *People* magazine. I combed through dozens of self-help relationship books, but I found them difficult to trust. Many are based on the author's personal opinion, or what so-and-so's great aunt did to land her husband back in the 1950s. Two of the bestselling dating books for women were not only written by men, but they were written by male comedians. I had to wonder if the advice they offered was valid or just another punch line. Would they one day jump onstage and say the joke was on us?

So I did what any good scientist would do: I started researching the biology behind love. Why is this question so important? Because once you understand how love works, you can make educated decisions. You will no longer be wondering, *I like him, what should I do now?* or *How long should I wait to have sex?* or *Geez, things seemed to have cooled off some, are we falling out of love?* You will know exactly what's happening and what actions to choose during each phase. And if things don't go exactly the way you hoped, you'll know what changes you can make.

Right now you might be wondering, "Why did a book like this take so long?" Allow me to explain.

# LOVE RESEARCHERS:
# SCIENTIFIC BLACK SHEEP

In 1975, former U.S. senator William Proxmire decided to make a name for himself by creating the Golden Fleece Award. This award was to be presented to any research project that Senator Proxmire considered a frivolous waste of taxpayer funds. Would you like to guess which project received the first Golden Fleece Award? In March 1975, Proxmire awarded the first Golden Fleece award to the National Science Foundation for spending $84,000 to study why people fall in love.[2]

Thanks to the Golden Fleece Award, the research on love became a type of scientific third rail. Love was considered such an irrational subject that researching it could jeopardize a scientist's career. Once a Golden Fleece award was given, the researchers' funding dried up. Therefore, any prudent scientist simply picked a less controversial subject.

Of course, there have been a few brave souls willing to risk poverty and public humiliation to conduct research about love, including anthropologist and science-of-love pioneer Dr. Helen Fisher of Rutgers University, who today is one of the most referenced scholars in the love-research community. I'm forever indebted to those pioneers. Thanks to Dr. Fisher, Dr. Arthur Aron, and others you'll read about here, I've been able to assemble the biochemical and neurological model of our pathway to real love.

Contrary to popular belief, love is not a mystery. Love is logical . . . or should I say *bio*logical? Not only does it make sense, but it follows a definite and specific four-step pattern. Improvements in research techniques, new equipment (such as *functional magnetic resonance* *imaging* [fMRI], which can locate love in an area in the brain), and openness on the part of the research community to study love have resulted in a flood of new information.

## LOVE IS A BIOLOGICAL NEED

What we call "love" is a biological drive. In fact, it's your greatest biological drive—in some cases stronger than any desire for power, property, and prestige. For example, imagine being the king of a great nation. You control vast sums of money and have immense influence and authority—but you must give it all up if you want love. Sound like the plot of some corny romance novel? Could love be so powerful that someone would give up abundant wealth and dominance for it? Could love trump other desires, such as prestige and safety?

It can, and it has. In 1936, King Edward VIII of England faced this decision. He was in love with Wallis Simpson, an American-born woman who was not legally divorced. Since her status precluded her from becoming queen, the prime minister gave King Edward an ultimatum—he could claim the throne or Mrs. Simpson, but not both.

Edward announced his decision to the world, saying, "I have found it impossible to carry the heavy burden of responsibility and to discharge my duties as King as I would wish to do without the help and support of the woman I love."[3] And, with that, the king abdicated his throne to marry his beloved.

Love is that powerful, but this story pales in comparison to the real power of love. Love is such a strong drive that without it, a person could actually die. As Helen Fisher says, "This drive for romantic love can be stronger than the will to live."[4]

## THE POWER OF LOVE

In the 1960s and '70s, American psychologist Harry Harlow performed a series of controversial experiments to test the theory that without love, we would die. Harlow decided to completely isolate an infant rhesus monkey from its mother. Rhesus monkeys are more mature than humans at birth, and unlike human infants, baby monkeys can move around on their own soon after birth. Harlow's experiments involved placing an infant monkey in a room with a surrogate, cloth mother. When the surrogate was present, the baby was observed exploring the room. However, when the surrogate was removed, the infant monkey would crouch, rock, and cry.

If the baby was left alone even longer, it entered a second, passive phase called *despair,* marked by inactivity, disinterest in the environment, a slouched posture, and the appearance of grief.[5] Harlow stopped the experiment. He realized that if left in the room alone any longer, the baby monkey might have died. He felt certain that this would have happened, even if the baby were given adequate food and water.

The monkey's reactions mirrored a similar depressive reaction observed in human infants, referred to as *hospitalism,* a deadly condition noted by Dr. Floyd Crandall in 1897. Dr. Crandall had been criticized for sending babies home to less-than-ideal hygienic conditions. He said his decision was "necessary in most hospitals to save the baby from hospitalism, a disease more deadly than pneumonia or diphtheria."[6]

Dr. Crandall observed that the death rate of infants under one year of age in hospitals was excessive.[7] Surprisingly, he realized that the better the hospital, the more likely the baby would die. This observation was counter to what would be expected. As Dr. Crandall noted, "It is difficult to understand why children placed in comfortable and beautiful surroundings should, after a time, begin to pine, and gradually waste away." He observed that the babies frequently died from marasmus—wasting away without the presence of organic disease. In other words, the babies were no longer sick, and there was nothing clinically wrong with them; they just died.

After close observation, Dr. Crandall realized the causal link. The deaths were most prevalent in larger hospitals. The larger and better-equipped hospitals had incubators, while smaller hospitals did not. In the smaller hospitals, the nurses were required to take turns holding the infants in their arms. Dr. Crandall figured out it was the lack of loving care, in the forms of holding and caressing, that was causing babies to perish. The infants had ample milk, warmth, and health care, but if they lacked love, they became lethargic and died.

In today's neonatal wards, parents are encouraged to take turns talking to and touching their babies. Incubators are equipped with sleeved gloves so the babies may be touched while a controlled environment is maintained. Anyone can provide a baby with the best medicine, the most nutritious food, and life-giving oxygenated air, but without that one essential ingredient of love, the baby could still die. The critical component for everyone to survive and thrive is love.

## HERE'S THE SHORT VERSION OF LOVE

The grand prize of love, the thing we're all hoping to find, is the euphoric sensation we call "falling in love." You feel happy and giddy. You might even feel like you've stumbled onto the key of happiness and you want to run around and tell everyone.

Falling in love is an actual biological state of mind. Although it feels wonderful, fMRIs show that the parts of your brain that are critical for your survival are actually deactivated. This is why you feel so great. It's also what causes you to know that you've just discovered "the one." This neurological anomaly helps you to be more vulnerable to your beloved.

However, the very phenomenon that causes important parts of your brain to shut down is what also makes falling in love so risky. Yet we seldom think it's risky, because it's such a strong biological drive. This dichotomy makes finding love difficult. On one hand you want and need it, while on the other hand, vulnerability to someone else makes it dangerous. If you fall in love with the wrong person (like so many do), you can get your heart broken.

To help keep you safe, Mother Nature provides natural biological obstacles to love. You can think of them as protective gates that only allow certain people in. These protective mechanisms are innate. Most are subconscious reactions that scrutinize anyone who tries to "get in." And if this isn't bad enough, these mechanisms are different for men than they are for women. When you don't understand what these mechanisms are, it can feel like the path to love curves through a land mine field. One false step and the whole thing blows up. The only people you seem to attract are not attractive to you. Or you think you had a great date, but he never calls back. It can be frustrating.

And it can get worse. Just when you think you've finally found the one you want to spend the rest of your life with, that enchanted feeling begins to wane. You see, the neurological state of falling in love is temporary. You can't walk around with important parts of your brain shut down forever. Eventually, you need to reach a state of homeostasis, of relative stability. When this happens, things can change, often in sudden and not-so-loving ways. Your critical judgment, which was suspended during the early stage of attraction, returns, and in some cases you wake up one day, look at your beloved, and think, *What was I thinking?* It's during this time period when most marriages in the United States end in divorce.

That's the bad news. The good news is that by reading this book, you will understand that love is not an event but a process with distinct biological phases. I'll explain what neurotransmitters (chemicals that help your cells communicate with one another) are involved. I'll explain that to fall in love, a woman has to have two neurotransmitters that build up to a certain level, while a man needs three. I'll explain what they are and how that occurs. I'll also explain how your behaviors can help or hinder the process. I'll also tell you what happens to you when you fall in love but, more important, what happens after you fall out of falling in love. Don't worry; it's not the end. I'll show you how you two can maintain lifelong love if you want to. I say *"if you want to"* because some of the cute memes, such as "we find love by chance, but we keep love by choice," are actually scientifically valid.

## UNDERSTANDING BIOLOGICAL LOVE

Your brain has three basic evolutionary layers. The innermost layer is the oldest. It's sometimes called the reptilian brain or ancient brain. Most animals, including birds and lizards, have this core. It houses instincts that drive you to seek survival basics, such as food, safety, shelter, and reproduction. If you've ever walked into a place and smelled something delicious, like fresh-baked bread or cinnamon rolls, and the next thing you know, you're standing at the counter with money in your hand, even though it goes against the diet you just committed to, your ancient brain was probably at the wheel. Your ancient brain can sometimes get you in trouble, but it's also the place where love begins.

The next layer is the emotional or mammalian brain. As the name implies, most mammals have this layer. In humans, it includes a structure called the limbic system, which houses emotions and memories. The limbic system contains important structures, such as the amygdala and the medial prefrontal cortex (mPFC). These structures are critical players on the path to love. In order for sexual attraction to become love, it must successfully pass through this minefield of emotions and memories to eventually reach the home of real love, the neocortex.

The third layer is the neocortex. *Neo* means "new" and *cortex* means "bark" or "layer." Because it's the outer layer, the neocortex is sometimes referred to as the "thinking cap." It's the last layer to evolve, and gives us the ability to think, judge, reason, and really love.

## Figure 1. The Brain

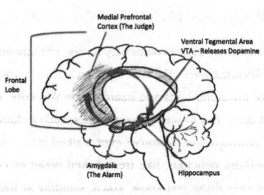

The shaded are is the limbic system. Arrows show reward circuit

## CRAZY IN LOVE

Before I started this research, I thought love was like a light switch, it was either on or it was off. Either you felt it, or you didn't. However, what I discovered is that love changes and evolves. Researchers use fMRI, a type of brain scan, to discover what part of the brain "lights up," or is employed, during different activities.[8] As you move through the phases of love, different parts of your brain light up or go dim.

At the same time, your neurotransmitters, those chemicals that allow the different parts of your brain to communicate with one another, increase and decrease. This can cause your head and your heart to feel dynamic emotional shifts. It can also cause your anxiety level to fluctuate, or should I say your "perceived anxiety" level. I say "perceived" because at the early stage of attraction, your stress hormones are extremely high, which normally would make you feel like a nervous wreck, but because the part of your brain that should be responding to the high cortisol level is shut down, instead you feel euphoric. The increased perceived anxiety at the beginning of dating can make you feel uncomfortable and eager to do something. In fact, it's this fluctuating angst that can make finding and maintaining love tough, because your feelings keep changing.

This chart shows the dramatic fluctuations that can occur as you move through the phases of love. I'll explain what you can do to mitigate these emotional upheavals, but first, allow me to explain what the four stages are.

## Figure 2. Fluctuations of perceived vulnerability during different stages of love

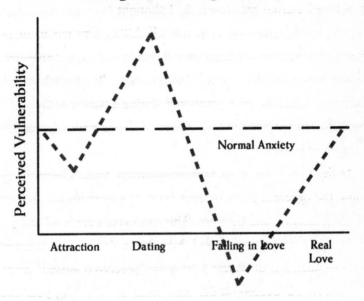

## PHASE 1: ATTRACTION

When you first meet someone new, the fMRI indicates activity in the ancient, more primitive part of your brain.[9] Attraction and desire begin in the center, or subconscious, region. Since this is not the thinking part of the brain, an attraction may not make logical sense. In fact, it may only make sense to your senses. That is to say, just as an alligator naturally moves into the sun to get warm, or into the water to cool off, you naturally move toward environments and people whom you sense are favorable. You're subconsciously pulled toward some people and repelled from others.

You feel this pull as a physical response. Your body tells you when it's sexually attracted to someone by releasing norepinephrine, a neurotransmitter that affects your sympathetic and central nervous systems (more on this later in the book). This makes your heart beat faster and your palms sweat. You feel excited. But this is just a momentary response of the exciting, norepinephrine-charged initial phase. At this point you have a slight dip in your normal anxiety level, which allows you to get a little closer to take a look at this new and interesting stranger.

## PHASE 2: DATING

Once your body registers an attraction, you can choose to act on it or allow it to dissipate. One way to act on it is to move into the next phase: dating. If you choose to move into dating, a new neurotrans-mitter, dopamine—the neurotransmitter of your reward center—comes into play. Every time you enjoy yourself with someone or while doing something, you produce dopamine. This trains your brain to know what you like. Most types of rewards—such as food, drugs, and sex—increase dopamine.[10] The increase is perceived as pleasurable and makes you want more.

During courtship, the pivotal point between sexual attraction and falling in love, other gender-specific neurotransmitters team up with dopamine, which is why your anxiety level increases. Falling in love is a big deal because you become extremely vulnerable to the other person. Because of this vulnerability, Mother Nature doesn't want you to fall in love with just anyone. As you get closer to falling in love, apprehension can increase, especially in men.

Dopamine is the common dominator between men and women. However, men and women fall in love differently. It appears that a woman falls in love when her dopamine and oxytocin levels reach a certain level. In a man, dopamine, vasopressin, and testosterone levels must increase to a certain level for him to fall in love (we'll define these hormones and explore how they affect the different stages of falling in love beginning in Chapter 2).

### Figure 3. How Women Fall in Love

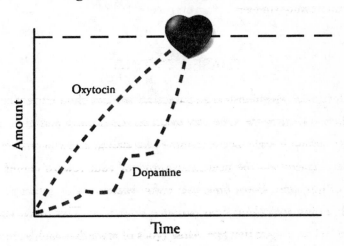

### Figure 4. How Men Fall in Love

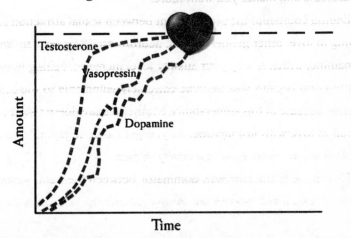

Since there are several different types of neurotransmitters at play in two different people, the effects they prompt do not always happen at exactly the same time. Because of this, love can be risky. It's during this courtship or dating phase that each person must grapple with his or her desire to take a risk on love. That's why the anxiety level is so high.

Being the first one to fall in love is dangerous. What happens if the other person doesn't reciprocate your feelings? You could suffer painful, unrequited love. This dating phase is fraught with danger, which is why most books are written about it. You want to try to understand what's happening in the other person's head.

Part of the problem is that men and women often make decisions based on their assumptions of others' intentions, or they predict the actions of the opposite sex based on how they themselves would respond. This is a big mistake. The differences between men and women go far beyond body parts. Each gender has unique brain chemistry and different needs, and each is under different biological pressures. Understanding how men and women typically react during the courtship phase can make dating easier, especially if the ultimate goal is love.

I'll explain how these chemicals accumulate in each person and how their behavior can affect how quickly they accumulate (or if they accumulate at all) as we journey through this book. I'll also explain the one thing that may make a man fall in love almost instantly.

## PHASE 3: FALLING IN LOVE

This third phase is often the one most people think of when they refer to love. This is the phase of mental instability, or the insanity of falling in love and losing your mind. This is where you become obsessed with your beloved, and, at the same time, blind to any of his or her faults. This is why you're so vulnerable. You also become nervous, excited, and even euphoric as you spend as much time together as possible, often in a horizontal position. This is the glorious phase celebrated by poets and philosophers.

Falling in love is a period of extreme vulnerability, but it doesn't feel like it, because Mother Nature has shut down parts of your brain that should be telling you to be alarmed. That's right. Allow me to repeat that: When you fall in love, important parts of your brain, sections that are critical for your survival, are taken off-line. This is why when you fall in love, your anxiety dissipates; all you feel is toe-curling euphoria and absolute certainty that you have just found "the one."

Many great love stories end with this phase—the knight wins the princess and they ride off into the sunset. However, this is not really the end. As enrapturing as falling in love can feel, this phase is short-lived.

But don't worry. There is another phase *after* falling in love. It's the glorious culmination of evolution—*real love*.

## PHASE 4: REAL LOVE

In the *real love* phase, love completes its neurological expansion. There is still some sexual passion activity in the primitive brain, but now the majority of the activity is in the prefrontal cortex—your higher brain.[11] Real love is calmer, nurturing, and more self-aware. An emotional transformation takes place. Now you're more concerned with giving than getting. This is the type of love that can last a lifetime. When you see the cute older couple sitting on the park bench, still holding hands after fifty years together, this is the type of love they share.

# CHAPTER

# MEN CHASE, WOMEN CHOOSE

I chose *Men Chase, Women Choose* as the title for this book because I was looking for the fundamental biological premise that governs relationships. In nature the rule would be males chase, females choose. But, of course, I needed to "humanize" it. No one would want to read a dry essay on the abstract science of relationships. You want to know how this applies to your love life, and to explain this, we need to start at the most basic level.

Turn on any nature show and you'll see the natural laws of courtship unfold before your eyes. You may see the bowerbird, so named because of the elaborate structure he builds called a bower. He spends weeks carefully constructing this stick-framed stage to entice the female. He decorates it with scraps of blue string and fabric, blue bits of plastic, like a blue straw or a candy wrapper, because he knows that blue is the female's favorite color. He also adds shiny bits of bling, if he can find some. If a female happens to show an interest and investigates, he begins his courtship dance.

She'll stand and judge him, as he genuflects, bows his head like an English gentleman of the court, then folds and twists his wings in a memorizing ballet. If she likes the dance (and the digs) she may stay, or she may fly from bower to bower looking for one that has just the perfect combination of stunning surroundings and exceptional performance. Only after she's fully satisfied will she allow the relationship to advance.

In a different corner of the planet, you can see male walruses in a bloody battle defending a tiny strip of sand. They lunge their massive bodies, which weigh about the same as an average car and are equipped with two-foot-long, body-piercing tusks, at any interlopers that dare cross into their territory. Battles can be frequent and can leave the dominant male with many battle scars. During these battles, the females lazily lie back and watch the spectacle unfold. They don't need to fight or worry. All they need to do is watch and then carefully choose the warrior they fancy.

All throughout nature you'll see mutated male appendages increasing in size to provide an advantage: interesting physical characteristics and adaptations that help males fight for dominance, which is often a precursor to courtship. For example, the massive headgear of bighorn sheep are used to battle competing males when females go into estrus. These massive accoutrements can reach up to 15 percent of the ram's body weight, weighing upward of thirty colossal, calorie-burning pounds. In addition, the horns can grow so long that they interfere with sight, forcing the rams to rub away the edges to see better.[12] In the fall, massive battles between males can be heard for miles as they bash horns in order to prove who the best "man" is. The male with the largest rack often wins the admiration of the females.

Horns are not the only male body part that have transformed in an attempt to fight for the affection of a female. The platypus, a duck-billed marsupial, has evolved a sharp ankle spur that's used to fight other males for dominance, while the Japanese Otton frog has evolved something that's usually only seen in comic book movie characters: a combat-ready fifth finger spike that's used to ward off other male suitors.[13]

Of course, these guys are not alone. Males of many species battle other males for the attention of females. Fights between males for dominance can be seen with whitetail deer, antelope, bison, rhinoceroses, and, of course, at the local college bar on a Friday night.

In most species males compete with each other to prove to a female which one is uniquely qualified for the job. Males perform tests of skill, fight other males, serenade, build alluring houses, provide food, and act like an all-around nice guy to attract the attention and the potential affection of females.

## NATURAL LAWS

Biologists study nature in hopes of discovering and defining laws. Laws are observations that hold true under every circumstance. For example, the law of gravity essentially says objects fall to the ground. Gravity affects everything on Earth and holds true in every situation.

Scientists look at a variety of natural phenomena to try to find patterns. When we find something in one species, we look to see if we find similar activity in other species. For example, many species migrate in the spring and fall. If we see a particular species heading south every year in October, we can make a safe prediction that this might be a migratory species.

Nature patterns tend to affect everything, including mammals, insects, birds, and humans. Like migration, there are other behaviors that are predictable between species. Some behaviors are so universal that we could make them into a law, like the law of gravity. Along that thought, if scientists were to establish a law for male–female relationships, particularly courtship, it could be "males chase, females choose."

Recently, another dating coach I know became upset with me. He liked to advise his female clients to go ahead and pursue a man. He felt a woman should be able to e-mail a man or walk up to him and introduce herself if she wanted to. In fact, he insisted that my idea that men chase was old-fashioned and no longer applicable.

I understood his logic. Society rules have changed quite a bit over the last decades. Women have much greater autonomy and can do just about everything a man can do, including chase. But as I'll explain in greater detail in Chapter 6, her chasing can have the unintended consequence of usurping his ability to fall in love.

For a woman looking for love, the golden rule is "men chase, women choose." But don't just take my word for it. Let's ask Mother Nature. She has especially built men for the chase—and built women to be choosy.

## HE'S BUILT TO PURSUE:
## THE GREAT AND MIGHTY TESTOSTERONE

Men are born with a very special, magical chemical that courses through their veins. This chemical has the ability to change and

shape their bodies into a lean, mean, chasing machine. The name of
this great compound is testosterone. Both men and women produce
testosterone, but almost all men produce much more than women do.
When looking at the differences between men and women, most look
at visual signs or secondary sex characteristics. For example, women
have breasts, fat layers that make them softer, and wider hips with a
slightly uneven gait that produces that "wiggle in the walk that makes
the world go round." Men, on the other hand, have bigger muscles,
narrow and solid hips, an Adam's apple, and facial hair.

Brains are seldom taken into consideration when we're looking
at gender differences, but just as hormones make our bodies look
different, the effect these hormones can have on the physical structures of our brains is just as dramatic. These neurological, structural
differences affect our behavior in rather predictable ways, especially
when it comes to relationships with the opposite sex.

## MEN CHASE: COMPETITION

Testosterone persuades males to compete for the attention of
females. Researchers have found that during courting, testosterone
levels increase in most animals, including humans. To confirm that
testosterone is linked to men's ability to woo women, researchers
from Wayne State University conducted an experiment. The study
engaged pairs of men in a seven-minute competition for the attention
of an attractive female. Precompetition testosterone levels were taken
and found to be proportional to the man's level of dominance. In
other words, guys that tended to "take control" of the conversation
or were more assertive had higher testosterone levels, whereas the
more reserved men had lower testosterone levels.

Next, the researchers observed the male's performance while competing for the woman's attention. They discovered that higher testosterone levels had an influence on the man's behavior. The men with higher testosterone levels were more aggressive toward the other competitors, showing dominance by denigrating the others.

Interestingly, at the same time, the woman reported that she "clicked" with the testosterone-laden men. The researchers concluded that the boost in testosterone provided an advantage during male rivalry, stating "our findings indicate that testosterone is associated with dominance behaviors and success when men compete for the attention of an attractive female."[14]

The potent testosterone provides males with the needed vigor to strive to win the ultimate prize—the female. But the desire to compete is not the only thing that prepares him for the chase. Just as his testosterone shapes his muscles and bones, they also shape his eyes and brain.

## PEEKING IN HIS HEAD

Researchers at the City University of New York compared the vision of men and women with respect to color and movement. They found that men have greater sensitivity to rapidly moving stimuli.[15] Men are better at spotting things that are mobile. In other words, if you want him to notice you, it helps if you're moving. That is to say, he's built to chase.

These visual differences make perfect evolutionary sense. Taking a look at ancestral roles, the primitive man's job was to hunt large animals. Back then he couldn't just walk into the local grocery store and plunk down a couple of bucks and stroll out with a brisket. No, he had to first spot and then capture his dinner. Movement acuity was paramount. He needed to see that slight twitch of a tail, as dinner was trying to hide behind a bush.

What this means when it comes to dating is that he's built to spot things that are moving, not standing in front of him, and then go after them. In other words, his vision prepares him for the pursuit.

But his vision is not the only anatomical difference that prepares him for the chase. He has several other structures in his brain that help him in his pursuit. One of the first places where you can see a difference between men's and women's brains is in the hypothalamus. The hypothalamus is a small part of the ancient brain. It's only about the size of a pea, but it's a critical structure when it comes to love. Not only is this tiny structure responsible for releasing the neurotransmitters needed for a man to fall in love, but it has a special spot called the "pursuit spot."[16]

## THE PURSUIT SPOT

Peering into a man's brain, we find he has an area in his hypothalamus called the *sexually dimorphic nucleus in the preoptic area* (SDN-POA), or "pursuit spot." This area of a man's brain is two and a half times larger than a woman's and is responsible for sexual response and the activation of male sexual behavior.[17] This little structure is what goads him into stepping up for the challenge and starting the chase.

Research shows that the pursuit spot receives a variety of sensory input and has direct connections to motor pathways.[18] In other words, when a guy spots a woman he's interested in, his pursuit spot says, "Oh yeah, go get her," then sends instructions to his feet to start moving in her direction.

The pursuit spot is the most conspicuous sexually distinct structure in the mammalian brain. It's so large in males that researchers are able to tell the difference between a male rat's and a female rat's brain by simply looking at the size of it.[19]

This pursuit spot is highly sensitive to testosterone. In one study, researchers found that if they castrated a rat pup, half his pursuit spot neurons died within twenty-four hours, making his brain look like a female's brain. By contrast, when the researchers gave androgens (testosterone) to a female, her pursuit spot grew as large as a male's.[20] In another study, researchers treated male rats prenatally with a substance that blocked the development of the pursuit spot in order to study the effects. They discovered that treated males showed less-masculine sexual behaviors, such as pursuits or mounts, and a reduced preference for a female over a male.[21]

A man's testosterone-supercharged pursuit spot makes him biologically predisposed and ready and willing to chase. When a man spots a woman he's interested in, he gets a jolt of testosterone. This in turn flips the switch on his pursuit spot. The next thing you know, he's standing next to her saying, "I couldn't help but notice . . ." His testosterone not only makes the pursuit spot in his hypothalamus bigger, it also changes the way he uses his hypothalamus.

## THE MALE HYPOTHALAMUS

Both men and women have a hypothalamus, but each uses theirs in a slightly different way. Scientists at the University of California, San Francisco, found sixteen genes regulated by sex hormones that were expressed differently between the sexes in the hypothalamus.[22]

The hypothalamus is subdivided into regions, with each area

having different functions. Both sexes have a dorsal premammillary nucleus (PMd) in their hypothalamus, but a man's is larger and contains specialized circuits to detect territorial challenges. The hypothalamus is activated during the exposure of a perceived threat, and the PMd plays a pivotal role in amplifying this process.[23] Like the walrus battling for his strip of sand, these specialized circuits in the hypothalamus make a man better prepared to acquire and defend his territory.

To confirm the theory that men are better at acquiring territory than women, a study at Stanford University School of Medicine conducted fMRI brain scans as groups of students played a video game. In the game, clicking balls accumulated points. In addition to the points, territory could be won or lost based on the position of the balls when clicked.

Researchers found that both men and women understood the game, and each wound up clicking on the same number of balls. The difference occurred in the amount of territory acquired. The men quickly realized which balls would provide them with the maximum amount of territory and began selectively choosing those balls. Women, on the other hand, didn't seem as interested in acquiring the territory.

An analysis of the brain scans revealed that the men's brains showed much greater activation of the reward circuit. In fact, the amount of activation was correlated with how much territory was gained, which was not the case for the women. In fact, the better connected a man's reward circuit was, the better he performed in the game. The researchers say that the findings indicate that successfully acquiring territory in a computer game format is more rewarding for men than for women. As they conclude, it makes sense that men are more prone to getting hooked on video games than women.[24] It's also why men are better at the chase. It's a primitive, almost subconscious response. Like the walruses and bighorn sheep, dominant territory-holding males usually have access to the most females. Of course, in humans, it's not a strip of sand or an open field, but men with bigger homes and more resources do tend to have an advantage when attracting women.

In addition to the tendency to acquire resources, men have another part in their brain that tends to be larger than women's and helps them to keep those resources: the amygdala.[25]

## THE MIGHTY AMYGDALA

The amygdala is the brain structure associated with fear and aggression. The size of the amygdala varies in accordance with the amount of testosterone circulating in a man's body. Scientists have found that hormone changes during adolescence create sex-dependent changes in the brain, making the amygdala volume increase significantly more in men than in women.[26] This size difference helps to explain the behavioral disparities seen in men and women.

A man's amygdala automatically scans the environment for any perceived threats. Because of his testosterone, a man's brain can be like a government military post. His larger amygdala is equivalent to a high-power satellite surveillance system. He can pick up the smallest threat and prepare countermeasures, which may even include a preemptive strike.

A woman, on the other hand, usually has a much smaller amygdala. Her amygdala is more like the local neighborhood watch—a kindly older woman who keeps a lookout to make sure the kids are safe. She settles skirmishes with milk and cookies, and stern warnings ("Now, stop that!"). If she ever actually detected a real threat, her plan of action would not be to strike but rather to call someone else for help.

As Dr. Joo-Hyung Lee, who studies gender differences in brain function at the Prince Henry's Institute in Melbourne, states, "historically males and females have been under different selection pressures which are reflected by the biochemical and behavioral differences between the sexes. The aggressive fight-or-flight reaction is more dominant in men, while women predominantly adopt a less aggressive tend-and-befriend response."[27]

The selective pressure that Lee is referring to is the ancient village life of the hunter and gatherer. In the ancient village, a man went out to do his hunting while a woman stayed at home to gather food and tend to the children. Everything was fine until one day when a group of strange men entered the village. The women had two choices: they could act aggressively or they could try to make friends with the strangers. Their best action was probably to be nice, serve them milk and cookies, and wait for the men to come back, because compared to the men, the women were not built to fight. The men, on the other hand, were better built to fight. So when they returned and saw their women with other men, their larger amygdalae sounded the alarm so loudly that they were ready to respond in seconds.

In addition to the amygdala, a man has additional brain structures that equip him to acquire and keep a woman, which we'll explore below.

## HIPPOCAMPUS

The limbic system contains a structure called the hippocampus. This little seahorse-shaped structure is part of the learning center and plays a key role in the formation of explicit long-term memory.[28] In addition to memory, the hippocampus is used for spatial navigation.

One study found that men and women use different parts of their brains to maneuver through unfamiliar environments. The researchers used fMRI to measure brain activity while men and women navigated through unknown, three-dimensional mazes. Subjects were instructed only to find a way out of the maze. The study found that men were significantly faster than women at finding the way out of the maze. Looking at the brain scans, both sexes had neurological overlap, but there were two important differences, namely, that women engaged the right parietal and right prefrontal area, whereas men recruited the left hippocampal region.[29] This means that women tended to think about where they were going, which may have slowed them down, while the men relied on a type of internal hippocampus GPS.

A research team at the University College London has discovered specialized grid cells in our hippocampus. These cells represent where an animal is located within its environment, something the researchers liken to having a satellite GPS in the brain. These cells were first discovered in a Norwegian lab in 2005, where researchers suggested that rats create virtual grids to help them orient themselves in their surroundings, and remember new locations in unfamiliar territory.

This operational difference between men and women makes evolutionary sense. If men were still clad in a loincloth, running out of the cave for a day of hunting, an internal GPS system would be critical. For example, say a prehistoric man spotted a succulent steak on four legs. In order for him to bring home his bounty, he may not just have to catch it, he might have to track his dinner for some time, venturing out over vast, unfamiliar terrain. Once he had tracked and caught his meal, he then had to remember how to get back home.

Having an internal grid system that functioned like GPS without having to think about it would've helped him achieve that. That automatic part was important, since he still had to contend with other animals that would try to steal his and his hungry waiting brood's dinner. Therefore, the man who had this ability would have had an advantage and would have evolutionarily been selected for.

But it wasn't just for being a good provider that Mother Nature may have created these traits; it appears that the quintessential player may have used his hippocampus to his advantage. Researchers at the University of Utah studied the behavior of three species of voles. One species was polygynous and the other two were monogamous and stayed by their mates' side. The scientists found that the hippocampus in the polygynous males was 11 percent bigger than that of the females of the same species, whereas the hippocampi in the monogamous males were about the same size as those of the females in that species.[30] The polygynous vole needed a larger hippocampus in order to keep track of, and find the locations of, all his fine, furry females. His increased sexual activity caused an increase of testosterone, which increased his hippocampus, which then helped aid his philandering.

Testosterone levels tend to be proportional to sexual activity, with more sexually active men and women tending to have higher testosterone levels. In one study, testosterone deprivation caused a 40 percent decrease in synaptic density in the hippocampus, while testosterone replacement in male animals normalized synaptic density. This is to say, testosterone tends to supersize a guy's hippocampus, helping him to remember where the women are.

Additionally, when male rodents were deprived of testosterone, their maze-learning performance was impaired.[31] Therefore, it appears that the polygynous vole's hippocampus evolved for both memory and navigation, increasing its size. Since he had more than one female, he had to remember where they were and how to get to them all. If you have a bunch of women to visit, you're going to need a bigger hippocampus tracking system to remember where they all live.

## WOMEN CHOOSE

In nature females are more selective because they take most of the risk when it comes to sex. Females must carry, give birth to, and feed the young produced. This is a huge responsibility that takes an enormous toll on health, time, and resources. If a female chooses poorly, she could potentially be doing all the work herself, putting her and her young at risk. If she chooses poor genes, she could potentially lose her children to illness. In order for her to have the best outcome possible, she must carefully scrutinize the myriad of applicants. Therefore, a female would never pursue a male. She would wait and carefully choose the best possible partner, as if her child's life depended on it—because potentially it does.

If we distill a male and a female to an elemental basis of one cell, we would have the egg and a sperm. The sperm is the only cell in the human body that's mobile. The egg doesn't have to worry about finding a sperm. She knows that all she has to do is sit tight, relax, and any second, thousands of eager sperm will be in the race of their life to find her. These sea-men are especially built for this competition. They have been working out, in the testes, in a type of "sperm boot camp," building stamina in the form of mitochondria for endurance to withstand the harsh environment in which the "female" resides. They have formed a specialized motility structure—the tail. They also come in force, wearing acidic helmets to break through the female barrier. It's a tough job, but they were born for this. Just like the egg, the female in her entirety doesn't have to worry if a male is coming. It's not a question of "if" but "when." I can confidently guarantee that you'll never see an egg putting on a short skirt or low-cut blouse, hanging out in the ovaries or running around the town's fallopian tubes trying to pick up random sperm. No, the egg knows she just needs to sit there as millions of excited little soldiers head her way.

The natural law of relationships is that the gender with the greater energetic investment in reproduction will be more discriminating when it comes to sex. Then the one with the least amount of energetic investment in reproduction will compete for access to the higher-investing individual. In most cases this means that males chase and females choose. However, this rule is not always drawn down gender lines. There are animals and insects out there where the male makes the larger energetic investment and is thus the choosier of the sexes. This is true of the bush cricket, sometimes called the "long-horned grasshopper."

When the bush cricket mates, the male provides the female with a massive ejaculate that she not only uses to fertilize her eggs but also partially consumes, using it for energy. His sperm can represent up to one-tenth of her lifetime caloric intake. However, as you might imagine, in the process of producing this gigantic sex snack, the male can lose up to a quarter of his body weight. Put in human terms, it would be the equivalent of a man producing fifty pounds of semen in one ejaculation.

Not surprisingly, male brush crickets are very choosy when selecting a female to mate with. He looks for the healthiest female he can find and rejects smaller females that may produce relatively fewer young. As a consequence of this gamble he takes by risking so much of his energy, females must compete for his attention. In this case females actually spend a great deal of time courting him, proving that they are worthy.[32] Since the gender taking the biggest risk gets to pick, in humans the woman does the choosing. And since she does the selection of different candidates, it means one wins while the others lose. But, more important, since she goes with the winner, it means she's the *prize*.

## WOMEN ARE THE PRIZE

As the prize, it's a woman's job to select the best candidate out of all the suitors vying for her attention. Therefore, Mother Nature has equipped her for this choosing. She has structural differences in her brain that are especially designed to help her pick. A woman's eyesight, unlike a man's, is designed to help her be choosier. Instead of grabbing moving objects, she's better at carefully picking out things based on subtle variations, such as hues.[33]

A woman's hippocampus is also used differently than a man's. Similar to the way testosterone helped the man to chase, estrogen helps her to choose. Researchers have found that estrogen can activate the area in the hippocampus responsible for many aspects of learning and memory. In addition, hippocampal volume increases significantly only in females.[34] Her hippocampus functions as a memory filer, sending memories to the appropriate areas for long-term storage and proper retrieval. This may provide women with better long-term memory. For example, compared to men, women recall longer and more detailed autobiographical memories, are more accurate at dating them, and are faster at recalling them.[35]

When you have to select from a number of suitors, you need to remember slight differences between them. That's probably why Mother Nature made a woman's hippocampus larger than a man's.[36] She remembers things, such as she likes suitor no. 1's hair, but she thinks suitor no. 2 is funnier, and suitor no. 3 has a nice voice. She needs to remember, sort through, and recall these differences and traits properly.

## OUR DIFFERENCES

The differences between men and women are important and necessary, because love and relationships are risky. The pursuer takes on a greater amount of risk in the beginning. Evolutionary biologists believe that men are hardwired to take risks for love. In a study conducted to see if men were inherently more willing to take risks once romantic elements were introduced, researchers discovered that men, but not women, were naturally inclined for these risks early on, and concluded that this tendency is rooted in evolution stating, "It appears that men have inherited this willingness to face dangers for women from our risk-friendly ancestors."[37]

Of course, both men and women experience risks in a relationship. But the timing and types of risks are different. Women take risks with becoming sexual. Therefore, in order for a man to experience excitement, he needs to take a different type of risk. His pleasure comes with the thrill of the chase. In other words, when a woman settles for something less than real courtship, both the man and the woman are robbed of this pleasure.

Now that I've hopefully convinced you that it's a man's job to chase and a woman's job to choose, let's get down to the business of love. But before we can get to love, we have to explore attraction.

# PART I

# **MEETING**

# CHAPTER

# ATTRACTION

One of my clients had a date, so I gave her a follow-up call the next day.

"How was the date?" I asked Whitney.

"Terrible," she said.

"Oh no, what happened?"

"Nothing really, that's the problem. He was sweet, attractive, and I liked him, but there was no chemistry."

No chemistry, no spark, or no buzz. Unfortunately, I hear that way too often. Everyone is looking for that mysterious feeling of being swept off your feet, that momentary intoxication called chemistry. Ever wonder what that feeling is all about?

## BEING SWEPT OFF YOUR FEET

God, I loved that feeling. I would go out searching for it like a bloodhound tracking her prey. Once I went to a dance with my friend and her boyfriend. I had just broken up with my boyfriend, so I was one of those awkward third wheels. Fortunately, that lonely awkwardness didn't last very long. A few minutes after walking into the dance, my eyes meet his. He was gorgeous, with thick, dark, curly hair and beautiful white teeth that were smiling at me. I smiled back, and it didn't take long for him to ask me to dance. He grabbed me in his arms, pulled me tight, then twirled and spun me around. We stared into each other's eyes and danced and swooned for hours. He was an amazing dancer, and the evening was magical. My friend's boyfriend came up to me afterward and said he'd never seen two people more in love. We had just met, but he swept me off my feet. Some would call this love at first sight.

## LOVE AT FIRST SIGHT

I will never forget that day. I was standing in front of a roomful of beautiful women, from sixteen to seventy-two years of age, with a variety of occupations and life experiences. Despite their diversity, they were all there for one reason: to find love. Many public-speaking coaches teach that speakers should start all presentations with a question, so that's exactly what I did. I asked these lovely ladies for a show of hands. "How many of you believe in love at first sight?" A bunch of hands shot up immediately, and as other women looked around the room, as if for permission, more hands went up. Soon, the room was a sea of raised hands. I thanked them and the hands went back down. I stood there for a moment (using the dramatic pause that public-speaking coaches recommend before making an important point) and then said, "What if I were to I tell you there is no such thing as love at first sight?"

I watched as the expressions on those beautiful faces wrenched into a tangled throng of disbelief. It was as if I had just announced to a roomful of kindergarteners that Santa Claus didn't exist. I felt the makings of a lynch mob, and at any minute I was expecting the back row to break out pitchforks and torches. I realized this was not the best way to begin a workshop, and I better do some fancy explaining before I found myself being showered with rotten tomatoes. But before I could begin, an elegantly dressed woman in her fifties spoke up in protest. She said, "I disagree. My husband, Roger, and I fell in love at first sight, and we've had thirty-two wonderful years together, until he died last June."

Several women looked at me with smug smiles as if to say, "Deal with that one, Professor Smarty Pants." I wiped the sweat from my brow and asked the sophisticated woman, "May I ask you a very personal question?"

She reluctantly nodded and muttered, "Yes."

"Did you sleep with Roger the first day you met him?"

"Oh my goodness, no," she snapped back.

"Thank you. You've proven my point," I said. "I'm not talking about attraction. What I'm talking about is the scam we've come to know as love at first sight."

You can know within minutes, or even seconds, if you're interested in someone. That interest can be the beginning of an amazing love where you spend a lifetime of bliss-filled years together. In fact, that's what this book is about. I want to help you find that exhilarating *I can't wait to get up in the morning so I can spend another day with you* kind of love—a rich, grounded type of love, *real* love.

Unfortunately, many of us (myself included) have created a mess out of our lives, as well as the lives of others, by instantly falling "head over heels," soon to be followed by "heels over head." Because of the way our brains are wired, we can become so convinced that we have just met "the one" that we don't think we need to date or even get to know him or her. We just dive right into the relationship and into bed, essentially short-circuiting the development of the true love we are looking for.

## THE BRIDGE STUDY

Imagine this. You're walking along a five-foot-wide, 450-foot-long, swaying, wobbly, wooden suspension bridge 230 feet over a raging river full of bloodthirsty, jagged rocks below. As you walk, you reach for the wire cable handrails, but they're too low to make you feel safe, and as you pull on them, they seem to give way, too loose for any real support. The wooden planks shift slightly as you venture into the center of this twisting passage. You're almost at the halfway point of this knee-buckler.

Just as you're starting to believe you might make it to the other side, you notice someone walking toward you. A very handsome man bounds along the bridge. His dark hair and shadow of a beard give him a rugged sexiness. You notice his wide shoulders and powerful chest as he closes the gap between you. You look down one more time. Any false move could mean certain death in the rapids below. You look back up and hear a voice. It asks, "Are you attracted to him?"

Sound crazy? But this scenario is the gist of the classic study conducted in the 1970s by researchers Donald Dutton and Arthur Aron. The aim of the study was to test if fear enhanced attraction. The researchers set up two different scenarios, one similar to the one I just mentioned and another with a low, solid wooden bridge built over a gentle, babbling brook, the kind of bridge you couldn't possibly fall off of, but if you did, the only real damage would be getting your shoes wet.

Dutton and Aron then tested the bridge walkers to see if the bridge had any effect on their level of attraction, specifically, sexual arousal. Dutton and Aron had several different men walk across the two bridges, with a woman meeting each in the middle. The woman was instructed to ask some questions and then, at the end of the encounter, give the gentleman her phone number. Next, the researchers counted which woman received the most calls. They found that two out of sixteen on the low, babbling brook called the girl. That's about 12.5 percent. But nine out of eighteen, or 50 percent, on the dangerous bridge called. This groundbreaking experiment found that fear magnifies sexual attraction.[38]

Now we scientifically understand why this happens. When you feel attraction, your body releases the neurotransmitter norepinephrine. Norepinephrine gives you that unmistakable feeling of attraction. You know the feeling—you meet someone you find very interesting and the next thing you know, your heart is pounding in your chest. It's pulsating so loudly in your ears you can hardly hear what they're saying. You notice that your vision narrows. You get a type of tunnel vision, blocking out other activity. You hope you don't have to shake hands, because your palms are so sweaty. You're terrified, nervous, yet magically enchanted all at the same time.

You feel like you're out of control, but at the same time, you're sweetly submissive, gladly accepting a ride on this magic carpet—wherever it may lead—hoping to travel to that mythical place called "happily ever after." Unfortunately, you're more likely to glide like the poor, ill-fated moth, dreamily drifting toward the light, destined for a painful demise.

## A LOOK AT LOVE AT FIRST SIGHT

I asked the lynch mob, "For those of you who raised your hands earlier and have experienced love at first sight, what did it feel like?"

One woman said, "I felt giddy."

Another said, "I had butterflies in my stomach."

"My heart was beating so loud, I was sure everyone could hear it," said another.

"I was nervous. My palms were sweating."

"I felt like I had tunnel vision. All I could see was him," said another.

"I felt really horny," a voice yelled from the back of the room.

I responded to all of them at once. "Perfect! Let's take a look at these responses. There were sweaty palms, focused vision, a fast-beating heart, increased nervous energy, and horniness. Can anyone tell me what these symptoms usually mean?" I asked.

"Besides the horniness, I would say fear," a voice called from the back of the room.

"Exactly," I said. "Those symptoms are indicators of anxiety and distress."

The feeling of love at first sight, or LAFS (yes, "laughs," because that's what nature is doing every time you fall for it) is caused by the release of norepinephrine as part of a biochemical fight-or-flight response. But instead of running away or fighting, Mother Nature is encouraging you to stay and have sex with this very interesting and attractive stranger.

Nature's original purpose for love at first sight was to encourage procreation. The lives of our hairy-knuckled, primitive ancestors were short in comparison to ours. They needed to grow up as quickly as possible in order to survive that vulnerable stage, learn how to find and/or kill food, locate a partner, and produce offspring—all in much less time than we have to accomplish the same. They were primarily concerned with fulfilling their basic need for food, water, and shelter because all these things directly aided their survival. There wasn't much time for long walks together on the beach; activities of this sort could equate to losing focus and being eaten by a saber-toothed cat. This period in human history was a stressful time, so Mother Nature gave the human race a hand, encouraging reproduction by linking sex to stress.

If you look at the history of humankind, it actually makes perfect sense. During times of stress, you'd want to fight or run and hide, and, oh yes, while hiding, eat and have sex. During times of crisis, such as war and epidemics, population replacement becomes critical. For example, some calculate that half or more of the European population was lost during the bubonic plague. Likely, with people dropping all around you, the last thing on your mind would be sex. But nature adds that additional bonus to the fight-or-flight response: sex as a response to stress, a way to ensure the species will continue under the least ideal circumstances. The next time you feel stress and have an inexplicable urge to eat carbs, or to have sex with the person next to you, you can chalk it up to the fight-or-flight response.

Not long ago there was a commercial on TV where a man approached a pet shop checkout to purchase two bunnies. The transaction took so long that by the time he was rung up, there were rabbits all over the counter, on the register, and even on the man's head. Rabbits are known for their prolific procreation, and abundant bunny-bumpin' love makes perfect biological sense. The more likely it is that a species will become food, the more that species will need to procreate for its ultimate survival.

The problem with this sexy fear response is that we're long past worrying about being someone else's food. The LAFS phenomenon —that is, the fight-or-flight impulse manifesting as an urge to mate— was important to our ancestors, but it has now outlived its purpose. It's an evolutionary vestige and like another vestige that most are familiar with—the appendix—it has lost most or all of its biological function. At one point in time, the appendix housed bacteria that helped us break down cellulose, or woody plant material. But since most of us no longer consume small branches, bark, or shrubbery, the appendix is no longer used for that. Although it is said to contain replacement bacteria, usually it just hangs out, off to the side of the cecum, not doing much or causing any problems. But for some, this evolutionary leftover can wreak havoc. An attack of appendicitis can have dangerous or even fatal consequences.

LAFS may be more likely to send you running to the nearest hotel than to the nearest hospital, but it can still cause considerable devastation. In fact, there may be some who would prefer an attack of appendicitis than ever again experiencing the consequences of LAFS.

## SIERRA'S STORY

I was having lunch with a colleague on campus. I told her I was concerned about a talk I was going to be giving to a bunch of women. I was worried because I was going to break some serious news to them: that there's no such thing as love at first sight; that it's nothing more than lust. She looked at me eagerly and said, "I'm so glad you're doing that. In fact, I wish someone had told me that years ago."

I closed my mouth, which had fallen open, and asked her to tell me more.

Sierra said, "I have to tell you, Dawn, if it happened to me, I know it can happen to anyone. It wasn't that long ago. I was already a doctor teaching here at the university when I met him. He worked for a medical supply company. I had seen him a few times, and we had mutual friends, but we had never really met. On a Friday morning, the company had a Danish-and-coffee meet-and-greet. It was my day off, but I decided to pop in. That was the beginning of the end. We hit it off instantly. He asked me to lunch. After lunch, we went parasailing and then to dinner. I was enamored and didn't want it to end. We spent the entire weekend together. Four months later we were married."

"I have to ask you something," I interrupted. "How long were you together before you two become sexual?"

"Well, that's the thing," she said sheepishly. "I'm a doctor. I should've known better. I mean, I teach this stuff to medical students. I'm afraid we spent the night together that first night. I got sucked into it. All the bad-match signs were there during the first month, but it was too late. I had fallen in love. [I'll explain how that can happen in Chapter 5: Love Potion]. We stayed married for seven years. I was the one who finally initiated the divorce. By then, I was a nervous wreck. I had become physically sick; I was even losing my hair. I learned the hard way about so-called love at first sight."

What Sierra learned the hard way was that even though she had believed it was love at first sight, she should've spent more time dating in order to determine if the two of them were a good fit. Blindly, she jumped into a sexual relationship, which caused her to lose her judgment. As she said, "The signs were there," meaning she knew that there were compatibility issues and trust issues, but because of the biochemical and physiological changes that occur when she fell in love with him, her judgment was foggy.

## YOUR BRAIN ON LAFS

The core of our brain, the ancient brain, sometimes called the reptilian brain, is believed to have been the first to evolve; it's considered to be the most primitive portion of our brain. It contains structures like the thalamus and the hypothalamus, which are responsible for our basic needs, such as food, water balance, sleep, pleasure, and sex. It's the part of the brain that's concerned with survival; in fact, if under attack, this small-but-mighty part of the brain takes control of the body, shutting down all systems that it deems unnecessary. When this part of our brain senses something that could negatively impact our chances of survival, like that saber-toothed cat, your amygdala (the brain's watchman) sounds the alarm, flooding your system with stress hormones.

Think of your brain as a fire station. You have a bunch of firemen milling around doing their day-to-day stuff, until that alarm sounds. Then all of a sudden, everything they were doing shuts down. They stop preparing food, stop playing cards, the television is shut down, and they jump on the fire pole and slide down. A similar scene plays out in our bodies, but instead of firemen, we have neurotransmitters.

All of a sudden, you feel supercharged, as if you had just chugged half a pot of coffee. Your heart beats faster, your blood pressure rises, your body pumps more blood to the skeletal muscles, and shuts down nonessential functions like digestion. Your body releases stores of glucose so you'll have ample energy to run away if needed—or, as you've probably guessed, to "fall in love lust."

Ironically, the reptilian brain also shuts down the conscious, or thinking, part of your brain. We have all been there. Something stressful happens and we literally can't seem to think. We get pulled over for speeding, knowing that if we get a ticket, our insurance will go up. We start feeling nervous, as stress hormones course through our blood. The police officer walks up to our window and asks, "Where are you going?" For a split second, our brain misfires. We start searching our mental catalog: *Where . . . where . . . where am I going?* For some reason, you draw a blank. You might even pause and say something like, "Wait. Let me think." Under stress, the thinking part—more specifically, the judgment part—of your brain disconnects.[39]

The moment is brief and you eventually remember, but researchers have discovered that too much stress can actually cause the nerve cells of the medial prefrontal cortex (mPFC), the evaluating part of your brain, to shrivel.[40] This is the area of the brain that predicts the outcome of an action. To make matters worse for our love life, researchers have learned that when people under stress are making a difficult decision, they may pay more attention to the upside of the alternatives they're considering and less to the downside.[41] So even though a part of our brain knows that a relationship with an escaped felon on the run might not be the best choice, another part of our brain is feeding us a list of reasons it will work, telling us how much fun it will be with just you and him in your new life together, running from the law and buying air fresheners in every town you pass through to cover up that strange smell coming from the trunk. Ah, sweet, neurochemical romance!

When norepinephrine floods our body, we have four prominent responses, sometimes referred to by students studying the effects as the four Fs: feeding, fleeing, fighting, and . . . well . . . having sex. Your brain is looking for relief. We can run away, fight, eat something, or take a powerful narcotic pain reliever in the form of an orgasm. Researchers have found that vaginocervical stimulation (like sex) releases a neurotransmitter into the spinal cord that's more effective, analgesically, than morphine sulfate when injected directly into the spinal cord.[42] In other words, when you have sex, you release a substance into your system that's more powerful than heroin.

This pain-relieving narcotic effect can make some women more vulnerable to LAFS. If a woman is going through a stressful and emotionally painful time, like I was when I met the guy at the dance, LAFS can become very alluring. Pain from a recent breakup, job stress, financial loss, or even a broken fingernail can send some women looking for the immediate relief promised by LAFS.

A woman may start the evening feeling bad, but soon she'll be all hopped up, feeling great, with the part of the brain that should be telling her to slow down and consider what's about to happen turned off. All she can see is the beckoning of a dreamy, narcotic-like, fairy-tale ending.

And there is another potentially significant problem with LAFS. Since the predominant neurotransmitter of lust is norepinephrine, the feeling of that supercharged biofuel coursing through the bloodstream is what comes to be associated with love. Your fight-or-flight response is meant to be only temporary. It's meant to be in effect just long enough for you to get to safety. In order to keep that "excited feeling" going, you need to keep triggering its release. This can result in a tumultuous relationship, with many fights that lead to a dramatic on-again, off-again, Tower of Terror ride.

A classic example of this is the celebrity marriage of Baywatch bombshell Pamela Anderson to Mötley Crüe rocker Tommy Lee. The couple met and married in 1995 after knowing each other for only ninety-six hours. The turbulent relationship lasted just three years.[43] Anderson didn't just file for divorce in 1998; she also filed charges of assault against her then husband because he had allegedly kicked her while she was holding their son, Dylan. Lee later pleaded no contest, was sentenced to six months in jail, and ultimately served four months behind bars.[44] After all this, it would seem logical to go their separate ways, but as with most norepinephrine-fueled relationships, the excitement of the drama brought them back together one more time after Tommy was released from jail. When asked about yet another reunion, Lee said, "We've only given it a try 800 times—801, here we go. Pamela and the kids have moved in with me. It's awesome. It's definitely working."[45] Unfortunately, as you've probably already guessed, numbers 801, 802, 803, and 804 didn't work.

One of the biggest tragedies resulting from these types of relationships may not be seen for many years. When children are raised in this type of turbulent atmosphere, they absorb this behavior early on and create a type of "love map." This love map serves as a blueprint that the child-become-adult will use to identify "love." This blueprint can start to take shape while the child is still a baby. Researchers have found that "The ability to trust, love, and resolve conflict with loved ones starts in childhood—way earlier than you might think. Your interpersonal experiences with your mother during the first twelve to eighteen months of life predict your behavior in romantic relationships twenty years later," says Jeffery Simpson, a psychologist with the University of Minnesota.[46] In other words, if you watch your parents break up and get back together over and over again, you become used to that pattern; it becomes your normal. Years later, when it's time for you to date, your brain identifies Mr. Swirling Tornado across the room and you jump into your storm-chaser van and take off on an exciting norepinephrine-infused adventure. Gee, thanks, Mom and Dad!

At this point in my talk, I usually have someone stand up and protest, "Now, wait a minute. Are you telling me that I need to run away from everyone I'm attracted to? Come on, Dawn. I came here for help with my love life. This is making it worse!"

I'm not suggesting that the way we find love is to avoid anyone you find attractive. The caution here is not to react to lust by jumping straight into a sexual relationship, which could complicate or even prevent your reaching your real goal. Now that I know you're not going to fall for love at first sight, let's take a closer look at attraction.

## OPPOSITES ATTRACT

One of the debates you often hear when it comes to dating is about if opposites attract or if people seek their own level. The answer to this perplexing question is both. You're naturally attracted to a combination of opposite and familiar. A union with someone of opposite or different genes will give your offspring a genetic advantage. The chances of having children with recessive diseases like sickle cell anemia, Tay-Sachs, and cystic fibrosis decrease the more your genes differ from your partner's.

At the same time, you're naturally attracted to someone who's familiar. Since attraction elicits nervousness, you're instinctively inclined to seek out safety in the form of something or someone that's familiar. It's a part of your innate survival mechanism. This may explain why people tend to choose mates who resemble themselves. As one study found, we are attracted to people with similar socioeconomic status and someone around the same age and the same level of intelligence and education. We also like similar personality traits, physical attractiveness, job interests, and, interestingly enough, someone with comparable body weight.[47] In fact, according to Elizabeth McClintock at the University of Notre Dame, "the strongest force by far in partner selection is similarity—in education, race, religion and physical attractiveness."[48]

"Sexual imprinting" is a set of familial characteristics that we pick up as children that shape mate preferences during adulthood. Experiments with birds and mammals have revealed that adults prefer sexual partners that are similar to the opposite-sex parent who reared them. Scientists believe that in early childhood, we internalize the characteristics of the people who raised us. Later, this shapes our choice in a partner, right down to what he or she looks like.

In a study comparing three hundred facial photographs of family members and controls, the subjects correctly matched wives to the husbands' mothers. A higher degree of similarity was perceived between the husband's mother and his wife than between the husband and wife. This may explain why all the significant men in my life had dark hair, hazel-brown eyes, and mustaches, just like my dad.

Of course, this could be a function of genetics; therefore, another study looked at emotional care in adopted families. They discovered that the more emotional warmth the father provided to his adopted daughter, the more visual similarity was perceived between him and his son-in-law. In addition, when a son experienced maternal rejection, they found a negative correlation between him and his spouse.[49] In other words, if a son felt love for his mother, he would choose a girl that reminded him of her, but if he had ill feelings toward his mother, he wouldn't want his wife to remind him of his mother.

Although physical similarities are relatively easy to measure, it's only one indication of a bigger imprinting phenomenon. That is, individuals fall in love with someone who reminds them of people who love them. This makes perfect biological sense. Everyone wants to feel safe and loved, so a person feels most comfortable with someone who looks like or acts like someone who make/made them feel safe and loved. Some people describe this comfort and familiarity as a "click" or "hitting it off." Because the person sitting in front of them somehow seems familiar in looks, values, opinions, or mannerisms, they feel a connection.

Although you look for the familiar, you're subconsciously opposed to dating people who are *too* familiar. A classic study that exemplifies this is the "kibbutz effect." A kibbutz is a type of communal-living environment and was started in Israel in the early 1900s. Children in the kibbutz were reared together in peer groups based on age, not biological relation. A study of the marriage patterns of these children later in life revealed that out of the nearly three thousand marriages that occurred across the kibbutz system, only fourteen were between children from the same peer group. Of those fourteen, none had been reared together during the first six years of life.[50] Since these children were encouraged to marry within their peer groups, the obvious aversion to the "too familiar" strongly suggests an instinctual, biological influence that was much stronger than the dominating social influence.

This opposite-but-familiar attraction can cause some seemingly unlikely combinations. The union of unlikely individuals may be one of the reasons we fall in love at all. But I'm getting ahead of myself. Let's continue by looking at the factors of attraction.

## FACTORS OF ATTRACTION

Norepinephrine heightens your senses, because it turns out that attraction starts with your senses. During the process of attraction, several seen, unseen, conscious, and subconscious factors come into play. As one researcher reports, "this attraction system operates in tandem with other neural systems, including the sex drive and circuits for sensory perception, discrimination and memory."[51] Our mind is judging potential partners based on myriad experiences, conditionings, and childhood memories. In addition, our senses are conspiring like a panel of expert judges. Just as Blake Shelton judges contestants on *The Voice*, our own ears judge potential mates' voices. Our nose is deciding if he or she smells good, while our eyes are giving him or her the once-over. As each of our senses detect these traits, they cast a deciding vote.

## THE EYES HAVE IT

I mentioned in Chapter 2 that a man is better at spotting moving objects while a woman is better at carefully choosing between things, but that's not the only difference in our vision. Men have 25 percent more visual cortex neurons than woman.[52] Because of their higher concentration of visual neurons, men tend to place a much higher value on visual stimulation than women. This makes the eyes the main gatekeeper of attraction, particularly for men.

In a BBC Internet assessment, men and women were surveyed for the top three desirable traits in a potential partner. The results were that women preferred honesty, humor, kindness, and dependability in men, while men chose good looks and facial attractiveness.[53] A man's initial focus was on things you could see. Men are particularly attracted to visual signals of fertility, good health, and good genes.

As Dr. Robert Provine at the University of Maryland explains, "Standards of beauty vary across cultures, however, youth and healthiness are always in fashion because they are associated with reproductive fitness. Traits such as long, lustrous hair and smooth or scar-free skin are cues of youth and offer the beholder a partial record of health."[54] Others add observable behaviors such as a sprightly, youthful gait and high activity level. Prior to modern medicine, pregnancy and childbirth was risky. Selecting a healthy, fit female was paramount to ensuring healthy children. Therefore, biologists believe that more than beauty, men have naturally evolved to look for clues of health, youth, and vitality.[55]

As Dr. Louann Brizendine points out in her book *The Male Brain*, men have been biologically selected over millions of years to focus on fertile females. What they don't know is that they've evolved to zoom in on certain features that indicate reproductive health. Researchers have found that the attraction to an hourglass figure—large breasts, small waist, flat stomach, and full hips—is ingrained in men across all cultures.[56]

## THE NOSE KNOWS

Next up on our biological panel of judges is the nose. Although we can be attracted or repulsed by someone's smell, we are not talking about cologne or bathing habits here. While those are important, pheromones are even more important. Pheromones are referred to as "ectohormones." *Ecto* means "outside," so these are chemical messengers designed to be emitted into the environment from one person that activate a specific physiological or behavioral response in another. Biologists have determined four specific functions of pheromones: menstrual cycle modulators that produce the "dormitory effect" or the synchronizing of the cycles of women living together, mother-infant bonding attractants, same-sex repellants, and, most important to this discussion, opposite-sex attractants.[57]

In most mammals, including us, there is a specialized pheromone detector called the vomeronasal organ or "Jacobson's organ," after the man who discovered it. This chemoreceptor is found at the base of the nasal cavity and is used by males of a specific species to detect the pheromones of females in estrus in that species. It has been found to have close connections with the amygdala and limbic system, the seat of emotional, hormonal, and autonomic control, but there are only indirect connections with the cerebral cortex, which is generally considered to be the site of consciousness.[58] In other words, this phenomenon of pheromone detection bypasses our conscious brain and acts directly on our emotions and motivation center. Therefore, a man can be affected by pheromones and never know it.

In a study using mice, researchers discovered that male mice with a working Jacobson's organ were more likely to take bigger risks when it came to love. The scientists believe that stimulation of Jacobson's organ by female pheromones activates the nucleus accumbens.[59] The nucleus accumbens is in the reward center and the main area of dopamine receptors, which become important in the next phase of dating or courting. Therefore, as female pheromones waft a male's way, it flips a switch, telling him to "go for it," because there is a prize nearby that he needs to win.

You may have seen male horses or other animals sniffing the air with their lips curled back. Scientists believe they are "tasting" the air. The act of curling back their lips provides better exposure to the Jacobson's organ, leading them to a receptive female. Humans don't necessarily do the lip curl, or wait . . . do they? Maybe that's why women got so excited when Elvis Presley did his famous snarl. In a way, his pulled-up lip was much like the male horse's. Like the horse, Elvis's lip curl sent the message that he was sexually interested, and he became a symbol that women loved.

Of course, most men don't stand around the local bar with their heads tilted up and their upper lips curled back, partaking of the aromas, or even take the Elvis side curl stance. But neither are they less affected by the scent of a woman. In a study from Florida State University, researchers had women wear T-shirts for three nights during various phases of their menstrual cycles. Male volunteers were then randomly assigned a T-shirt to smell. They were given either a T-shirt worn by a woman for three nights or a new non-worn T-shirt as a control. Saliva samples were collected both before and after the men smelled the T-shirts and then analyzed for testosterone. By the way, an increase in testosterone is an indicator of sexual attraction in men. This is important to remember, because pheromones are not the only way to increase his testosterone. This testosterone boost is below his conscious awareness, but once it's raised, he feels it as attraction (I'll explain more about this later).

The results of the study found that men who smelled T-shirts of ovulating women produced an increase in testosterone, whereas the men who smelled the T-shirts worn by non-ovulating women or non-worn shirts did not have an increase in testosterone. In addition, after smelling the shirts, the men were asked to rate the T-shirt odors on pleasantness. The men who smelled the shirts worn by ovulating women ranked those as the most pleasant smelling.[60] One group of pheromones produced by ovulating women is called copulins. As the name implies, their job is encourage copulation. Therefore, when Ms. Ovulating walks by a guy, she gets his attention when his own body gives him a testosterone nudge. The next thing he knows, he's following her around with an Elvis Presley lip-snarl grin, thinking, "Wow, there is just something about that girl."

## SHE NOSE

Men are not the only ones who use the nose to choose a mate. A woman also uses her sense of smell for choosing the best mate, but her nose has slightly different selection criteria. Studies suggest that health may be detectable. One study found that female mice could detect the males infected by parasites and avoided mating with them.[61] In another study, female butterflies could detect inbred males and avoided breeding with them.[62] In a different study, scientists studying stickleback fish discovered that females are attracted to males with a particular protein fragment. These fragments indicate which major histocompatibility complex (MHC) molecules he has. MHC molecules are small protein molecules that are part of the immune system. MHC molecules are used to fight disease, so selecting a mate that will provide her offspring with the best mix of immunity genes is critical.[63]

There is evidence that humans also have MHC-dependent mating preferences. One study found that humans prefer the body odor of MHC-dissimilar individuals. In the study, forty-nine women and forty-four men were MHC typed. Next, the researchers asked the women to rate the attractiveness of the odors of the T-shirts worn by the three MHC-similar and three MHC-dissimilar men. Women generally preferred the odor of the MHC-dissimilar men, describing them as "more pleasant." Moreover, the scent of MHC-dissimilar men was twice as likely to remind women of their mate's odor.[64] This would make evolutionary sense. A couple's offspring are provided the greatest survival advantage when opposites combine, providing the child with a stronger immune system. This adds to the debate that opposites attract.

## AN EAR FOR LOVE

Next up on our all-star panel of judges is the ear. Research shows that men prefer females with a high-pitched, breathy voice and wide formant spacing, which tends to correlate with her smaller body size. Women, on the other hand, prefer low-pitched voices with a narrow formant spacing, which suggests a larger body size.[65]

Women not only prefer low-pitched voices in men, one study found that a man's bass vocals might actually help a woman remember him. In the study, women were shown several images of objects while listening to the name of the object spoken by either a high-pitched or low-pitched voice. The women were then shown two similar, but not identical, versions of the objects and asked to identify the one they had seen earlier. The researchers found that women remembered objects more accurately when they had been introduced by the deep male voice. The researchers concluded that this was evidence that "evolution has shaped women's ability to remember information associated with desirable men."[66] The deeper voice is usually associated with the more dominant or alpha male, so nature has helped equip a woman to better remember him. Maybe that's why it's so hard to forget the singer Barry White.

Speaking of Barry White, it appears that music has a huge effect on a woman's sense of attraction also. In a study in (where else but) Paris, the city of love, researchers tested the effects that romantic music had on a women's willingness to give out her phone number. The researchers separated a group of women into two waiting rooms.

One played "neutral" music while the other played a soothing litany of romantic ballads. They then asked the women to move to a different room to discuss food products with a young man. When the experiment was over, the young man, using a standard line, would ask the woman for her phone number. After all the women had gone through, the researchers tallied the responses. They discovered that the young man was able to get phone numbers from 28 percent of the women in the neutral music room, but he almost doubled his chances with the women who had been exposed to the romantic music: 52 percent.[67]

But, guys, if you really want to get a woman's phone number, there is one more thing you can do to increase your chances. A study found that women were 31 percent more likely to give their number to a man carrying a guitar. That's double the amount of women who would give their number to the same man when he was empty-handed. Interestingly, the researchers tried a few more items and found that if the same man held a sports bag, his success dropped even further than the empty-handed guy.[68] Therefore, guys, ditch the gym bag, grab a guitar, and start playing romantic love ballads that you sing in a deep Barry White timbre, and you should be going home with more numbers than the phone book.

## SOUNDS LIKE LOVE

Interestingly, the way you speak might actually determine if your relationship is heading toward love. Researchers at Albright College found that people engage in voice modulation when speaking to a romantic partner versus a same-sex friend during phone conversations. In the study, researchers recruited people who were newly in love and asked them to phone either a romantic partner or a same-sex friend. In the brief conversation, the participants were instructed to simply say, "How are you?" and "What are you doing?"

Next, the researchers played the recordings to eighty independent raters who judged the samples for sexiness, pleasantness, and degree of romantic interest. The study found that the raters were able to correctly identify whether the caller was speaking to a friend or a lover. This led the researchers to conclude that people alter their voice to communicate relationship status.

Next, the researchers used a spectrogram to measure pitch. They found that both men and women tend to match the pitch of their romantic partner. The researchers believe that this change in voice represents a desire for affection and intimacy, and is a way of telling the other person "I am one with you."

The researchers then performed a paralanguage analysis. Paralanguage samples are stripped of their content but maintain inflection and intonation. The researchers were surprised to find that the raters could sense stress and nervousness when the callers were speaking to their lovers.[69] The researchers might've been surprised, but after what you know about attraction, you shouldn't be. When the callers phoned their romantic partner, they were just simply attracted and hopped-up on norepinephrine.

## IT FEELS LIKE LOVE

Jana was perplexed. She had been talking with Christopher for weeks. They had their first coffee date last week and she was beginning to like him. But this week they met again and she walked away with a totally different impression of him.

"I don't know what happened. The first time we met, he seemed nice, warm, and generous. However, this last date, he acted the same but somehow seemed rather cold and aloof," she said.

"Tell me more about the date. Where did you go?" I asked.

"Well, the first time we just met for coffee at a cute little shop near my house and just chatted for about an hour. He told me about his work and hobbies. We have some common interests and it was nice," she said.

"What happened on the next date?" I asked.

"Nothing really different, except we met for frozen yogurt. I had cake batter with Reese's pieces, and I think he had mocha. We talked mostly about playing golf," she said.

"What did you have on the first coffee date?" I asked.

"A pumpkin spice latte," she said.

"Was it hot or cold?"

"Hot . . . why?" she asked.

Jana's two very different impressions of her date might be the result of her hands casting a vote. That is to say, the settings and what a person feels with his or her hands can have an effect when it comes to attraction. Tactile sensations are an important way to gather information from your surroundings and can have a profound influence on how someone senses the environment and the people in it.

In a unique experiment by Lawrence Williams at Yale University, Williams set out to discover if temperature had an effect on perception. He believes that it's no coincidence that we use the same word—warmth—to describe both a physical and an emotional experience. "Somewhere in the brain, those two sensations are linked," he says. "Think of a baby held in its mother arms. The child is experiencing love, affection, and comfort. But you also have, at the same time, an experience with a warm object, in this case a warm human being."[70]

To test his theory, Williams had the participants of the study greeted by a host prior to getting on an elevator. The host held a cup of coffee, a clipboard, and two textbooks. Not realizing they had started the study, during the elevator ride, the host would ask the participants to hold either her hot cup of coffee or iced coffee as she jotted down some notes. After she wrote down the information, she took back the coffee.

The participants were then directed to the experiment room, where each read a story about a hypothetical person. The participants were then asked to rate the person on ten personality traits. The experiment found that people who held the hot cup of coffee perceived the hypothetical person as warmer, more social, happier, generous, and better natured than those who had held the cup of iced coffee. In contrast, the participants who held something cold perceived the hypothetical person as cold, stoic, and unaffectionate.[71] Therefore, on Jana's first date, when she had the hot pumpkin spice latte, she walked away believing that Christopher was a nice, warm, and affectionate guy, but on the second date, when holding the frozen yogurt, her impression of Christopher literally cooled.

It's not only our hands that make this perception, but our legs, arms, and even our butts can chime in their opinion. Massachusetts Institute of Technology researcher Joshua Ackerman calls this "incidental haptic sensations"—the phenomenon where physical touch can affect your perceptions. In his study participants judged impressions by the seat of their pants. Eighty-six participants were asked to sit in either a hard wooden chair or a soft-cushioned chair while completing an impression formation task, where they were asked to judge an employee. The study found that chair hardness had an effect

on this judgment. Participants sitting in the hard chairs had perceptions of strictness, rigidity, and stability, while participants sitting in
the soft sofa had a more positive overall impression.[72]

When Jana had her initial coffee date, she held a warm cup of
coffee and sat on a cozy couch, causing her to feel that Christopher
was kind, comfortable, and warmhearted. However, on the next date,
when she went to the yogurt shop and held the frozen yogurt while
sitting on a cold stiff plastic chair, her impression of Christopher
changed. Now, instead of warm and friendly, Jana perceived him as
cold, harsh, and quite literally a bit of a rigid hard-ass.

## THE FIRST KISS

Before someone can pass into love, there is one test they have to
pass—the infamous first kiss. Although tempted to call this the taste
test, the first kiss actually has several factors involved, including taste,
smell, appearance, and feel. In a joint study involving more than
a thousand college students, researchers evaluated the preferences
and attitudes of kissing. The study found that men place a value on
kissing, but women place a higher value on the first kiss and actually
use it as an assessment device to determine if the man is someone
they would like to see again.

The study found that women judge a good kisser before they even
kiss by looking at the appearance of his teeth. If he has a nice smile
and white teeth, chances are more favorable that he'll move to round
two: the kiss. At the moment of a kiss, there is an exceedingly rich
and complex exchange of tactile and chemical cues, such as breath
and the taste of the mouth. This magical moment is critical and may
mean the difference between love or not.

In a Gallup poll (cited in the same study) people were asked, "Have you ever found yourself attracted to someone, only to discover after kissing them for the first time that you were no longer interested?" Of the respondents, more than half the men, or 59 percent, said "yes," while a whopping 66 percent of the women said "yes."[73] Therefore, that first kiss may mean the difference between moving on to the next romantic phase or having the door of love shut in your bad kisser. To ensure your favorable ranking on the kiss-o-meter, may I suggest forgoing the garlic risotto and maybe packing a few mints on your first date?

Oh, and one more interesting thing: the part of the brain that becomes activated during first kisses is the insula. The insula has an important role on the road to love. Its job is to take senses and assign emotional significance to them. The insula is involved in sensations such as touch and taste, as well as feelings of trust, empathy, and love.[74] It's important to keep the insula happy, because, as a Yale University of Medicine Study verified, it's also involved in the experience of emotions as disgust.[75] Therefore, when the insula makes a negative judgment because a cup is cold or a seat is hard, it can cause the person to walk away, feeling repulsed. And because the insula is linked with taste, a negative encounter can literally leave a bad aftertaste in his or her mouth. Yuck! But then again, if the experience is favorable, the date can foster feelings of trust and empathy, as well as literally being sweet.

In a joint study with Singapore and the Netherlands, researchers investigated the effect that emotion had on taste. They had a group of people sit down and write about a personal story either about romantic love or a really boring essay on landmarks in Singapore. Afterward, they asked the participants to taste candy samples consisting of sweet-and-sour drops or bittersweet chocolate samples. The people who wrote about love rated their samples as sweeter than the landmark group.

To further test the theory, the researchers repeated the test, but this time, instead of candy, which is inherently sweet, they decided to use distilled water. Again, they primed the participants by having them write about love, or this time, happiness. Again, the researchers found that the participants who wrote about love rated the plain distilled water as sweeter than the participants who wrote about happiness. The researchers believe it's because we have a shared neural circuitry associated with experiencing both love and sweetness. As the saying goes, "neurons that are wired together fire together." Therefore, it's possible that when one experiences love, it activates areas associated with sweetness, eliciting a sweet sensation even without actually tasting it.[76] In other words, if the night is going well as thoughts of potential love come up, that good-night kiss could be "sweeter than Tupelo honey."

Now that you understand a little more about what's behind that feeling of attraction, let's take a look at what you can do to enhance your attractiveness to draw love in.

# THE ART AND SCIENCE OF ATTRACTION

$F$ive foot seven inches tall, early thirties, with sun-kissed skin and long blond hair, Christy didn't have any trouble attracting men. Like the majority of daters in the United States, Christy joined an online dating service. She relished coming home after work to peruse profiles and read her most recent e-mails. Christy is not alone. According to recent statistics, 40 million of the 54 million singles in the United States have tried online dating.[77] Although she met several men, she just didn't seem to feel a connection with any of them.

One day, Christy's friend Carla suggested that she go on a blind date instead. Carla worked with a guy named Matt who she believed would be perfect for Christy. Unfortunately, after Carla showed Christy his picture, Christy became reluctant.

"He was not the kind of guy I would normally pick," Christy admitted.

However, with Carla's insistence, Christy went on a coffee date.

"I figured, what could getting a cup of coffee hurt?" she said.

To her surprise, she hit it off with Matt immediately.

"He was funny and charming, and we had so much in common," she said.

The two started dating, and within a year they got engaged. Christy's experience is not surprising. We actually use different parts of our brain when judging a potential date from a photo as opposed to in person. Researchers conducted brain scans of volunteers looking at pictures of potential dates. The researchers found that two brain regions became active while volunteers viewed the photos. The paracingulate cortex calculates how attractive the person is, while the dorsomedial prefrontal cortex decides if it's a person they would like to pursue a relationship with. After the initial viewing of the pictures, the researchers then had the volunteers meet. They discovered that when the two people met, a second region became active. The rostromedial prefrontal cortex began making more sophisticated calculations, such as how similar and likable the person was.[78] Therefore, some people may be dismissed as potential partners based on pictures, but if they met in person, they would be considered desirable. The reverse is also true. A person can become quite enamored with a photo, but once the two people meet in person, those feelings can disappear faster than promises after Election Day.

## WHAT THE HELL DOES SHE WANT?

Attraction is so undiscerning that you can be in love with someone and still find yourself attracted to someone else. That's the funny thing about attraction. It really doesn't tell us much about what we want when it comes to love. Quite often the characteristics that someone finds initially attractive are not the same ones he or she chooses for a long-term relationship.

For example, in one study women were more attracted to a man who purchased a bright-colored, flashy car—such as a stereotypical, midlife-crisis, red Porsche—than one who purchased a Honda Civic. But there was a catch. Although the women found the Porsche guy more attractive to date, he wasn't preferred as a marriage partner. As the report noted, "When women considered him for a long-term relationship, owning the sports car held no advantage relative to owning an economy car."[79] Therefore, although a woman might like to go on a date with a man in a Porsche, she probably wouldn't date him for very long.

The Porsche example is one of the things men complain about. I've had men ask me, "What do woman really want?" Wonderful, sweet, and loving men are completely frustrated because they are trying to please a woman and be the man she says she wants—and there's the problem. She really doesn't know what she wants. Oh yes, she'll tell you she wants a sweet, kind, and sensible man. But, just like the Porsche study, she walks right past Mr. Stable and Sensible and runs off with the guy in the flashy red car.

The poor, sensible car guy is left shaking his head, exclaiming, "She said she wanted stability, what gives?" Initial attraction is what gives. The majority of women will tell you that they want a nice guy. Most women will not check the box indicating she wants a man who's grumpy, unpredictable, or irresponsible. But although she says she doesn't want that type of man, what she says and what's she does, or who she picks, can be very different.

Most people indicate that positive emotional traits and a nice personality are desirable in a relationship partner. However, a study from the University of British Columbia asked the participants to rate pictures based solely on gut sexual attraction and not which person would make the best boyfriend or girlfriend. The study, in which more than a thousand participants rated sexual attractiveness of the pictures, found that women were least attracted to smiling, happy men. Contrary to what women say they want in a relationship, these women were more attracted to men who looked proud and power-ful or moody and ashamed—characteristics often displayed by the iconic "bad boy" types.[80]

Why this discrepancy? That initial, exciting spark of attraction is mostly about the sex drive. We are attracted to what we feel is sexually desirable. Anthropologist Helen Fisher states that the actual feelings an individual experiences as he or she becomes attracted to someone is a product of the evolution of the mammalian brain, which is designed to enable individuals to choose genetically supe-rior mating partners.[81] In other words, we are designed to be attracted to the best person to have sex with, not to have a lifelong relationship with. That's the reason I start every dating coach client with a list.

## THE LIST

Before a person starts to date, I ask them to sit down and com-plete a list. The list consists of everything they want in their ideal partner. If they want someone who's tall, they put it down. If they want someone who's educated, they write it down. If they want a dog lover, they write it down.

Next, I ask them to write down their deal-breakers. Deal-breakers are things that the person possesses that would make you not want to begin a relationship with them (for example, one of my deal-breakers was drug use). After they have a complete list of everything they want and everything they don't want, I ask them to trim the list. They need to pick out the top five things they want, or the "must-haves." Then they must pick out the five things they don't want (the deal-breakers). Everything else on the list is negotiable.

This list serves two purposes. First, a person identifies their most important criteria for choosing a mate. As the Porsche experiment revealed, what a woman wants and what she picks are often vastly different. Attraction starts in the primitive brain, but when you make the list, you're using the more advantaged part of your brain—the neocortex—and making decisions based on well-thought-out wants versus primitive desires. This is important to know, because as you start to date, as you already know, attraction can short-circuit the more advanced brain. When this happens, without a strong conviction, you're more vulnerable to lusty spur-of-the-moment decisions.

The list can help prevent regret. When you know what you want and agree upon those desires ahead of time, it can stop you from running off with someone who's geographically undesirable just because they have a cute butt.

Now that you know what you want, you need to learn how to attract it. Since, more and more people are meeting online, let's begin this discussion with your dating profile.

## DATING PROFILES

Online dating is a great way to meet someone. But with so many options, people don't tend to give each individual profile very much time. In fact, the majority of online daters tend to scan the profile pictures. Making your profile picture selection is a potential critical step on your road to love.

When I started working with Candace, I asked her what she felt her problem with finding love was. She replied, "It seems like all the men I meet are only interested in a sexual relationship."

When I saw her online profile, I realized why she attracted those types of men. Candace is a very attractive and fit woman. In fact, she does health and fitness work for a living. Because of her work, she has lots of pictures of herself in tight and revealing clothes. Unfortunately, she chose a sexy, full-length, figure-hugging photo for her main profile picture.

Researchers believe that men focus on different things depending on the type of relationship they are looking for. One report states that men who are looking for short-term companionship are more interested in a woman's body than those looking for a long-term relationship. Those who are pursuing a long-term relationship focus on a woman's face. As one researcher put it, "men's priorities shift depending on what they want in a mate, with facial features taking on more importance when a long-term relationship is the goal."[82]

By putting a sexy body shot as her profile picture, Candace unwittingly attracted the more casual relationship-minded men. Therefore, we simply replaced several of her body-shot pictures with face shots, and we quickly noticed a change in the caliber of men who began responding.

In selecting the right profile picture, there are several things that you can do to increase your attractiveness. The first is using the color red. Red has had a direct connection with sexual attraction for thousands of years. That's one of the reasons you see so much of it on Valentine's Day.

Researchers have found that the color red enhances our attraction to another person. At the University of Rochester, psychologist Daniela Niesta conducted a study that measured men's attraction to the same woman. She showed the woman's picture to the men but varied the background color or the color of the woman's shirt. Niesta found that men were most attracted to the pictures that included red.

Next, Niesta told the men, "Imagine that you are going on a date with this person and have a hundred dollars in your wallet. How much money would you be willing to spend on your date?" Not surprisingly, Niesta found that men would spend the most money on a woman in red.

Now, you might be wondering if red has the same effect on women. Another researcher, Andrew Elliot at the University of Rochester, decided to test the effect of red on women. He asked a group of women to rate the pictures of men whose shirt color was digitally altered. Elliot found that the women also rated the pictures of men wearing red as more attractive. But, even more interesting, he found that without actually meeting or talking to the men, the women perceived the men in red as having a higher social status, more likely to make money, and more likely to climb the social ladder. But there was one other thing that may have the guys running out for a new red shirt. Elliot found that the women in the study also perceived the men in red as more sexually desirable. Not only that, but the women were more willing to date, kiss, and even engage in sexual activity with the men in red.[83] Therefore, your initial profile picture should have you either wearing red or it should have a red background.

Next, let's take a look at the face. Both men and women have asked me what people are most attracted to. We live in a beauty-conscious society, and this can cause some people to feel intimidated. Some worry that they look too average. The good news is that average is a great thing. Research from the University of California, San Diego, and the University of Toronto wanted to discover which facial features people were most attracted to. In four separate experiments, they asked participants to make paired comparisons of attractiveness between female faces with identical features but different eye-mouth distances and different distances between the eyes. The researchers discovered something they called the "golden ratios," the most attractive distance between the eyes and mouth and the best distance between the eyes. Interestingly, these proportions correspond with those of the average face.[84]

However, you still want to put your best face forward. To do that, may I suggest a picture showing your left cheek? According to a study from Wake Forest University, images of the left side of the face are perceived and rated as more pleasant than pictures of the right side of the face. Researchers have theorized that the left side has a greater intensity of emotion, which the observers find aesthetically pleasing.[85]

As you pose for your left-cheek picture with the red background, there is one other thing you need. In fact, this may the most important thing you can do to attract love in your life. What is this key to love? A smile.

If you're a woman, the single most important thing you should be doing to attract love in your life is smiling. Remember the perceived vulnerability? When you smile, you seem friendlier and more approachable. Pictures of smiling women get more attention. But this only applies to women. Ironically, smiling men get less attention online. Women tend to go for the moody or proud and powerful. Now, if you're a man, and you're not sure if you can pull that off, grab that guitar I told you about in Chapter 3.

## THE SIX ESSENTIAL ELEMENTS
## IN AN ONLINE DATING PROFILE
## IF YOUR GOAL IS LOVE

♥ Include at least three photos: one of yourself wearing red, another with a left cheek exposure, and a full body action shot (no bathing suits).

♥ Start with a description of yourself, not what you're looking for.

♥ Do not include anything negative, such as "still looking" or "single again."

♥ Include interesting and unique features about yourself. Did you run off to join the circus when you were a kid? (Uniqueness stimulates a dopamine response in the potential date. You'll see why this is so important in Chapter 5.)

♥ Include fun activities. Do you like to surf, collect antiques, or hike? (No walks on the beach, please.)

♥ Let potential dates know you're serious. Do not click the box that says "Looking for friends."

## YOU NEED TO MEET

Once a woman starts chatting with someone online, she wants to make sure she sets up an off-line date rather quickly. According to a study conducted by Dr. Paul Zak at Claremont Graduate University in California, humans release oxytocin, also known as the "love hormone," while communicating through social media websites, instant messaging, and text messaging. "The brain doesn't really distinguish between real interaction and texting," says Zak.[86]

Although both men and women produce oxytocin during these times, as I'll explain in Chapter 5, it only causes women to fall in love.

Therefore, a woman can be texting away, certain that he's "the one," and even falling in love before she meets the man. But when *he* meets *her*, biologically and chemically speaking, he's *just* met her. His body is responding to her like it's the first day they met, because, well, for him, it is. She may have developed warm and loving feelings for him, but he needs to see her in person to get the ball rolling.

This may be why, according to the University of Texas School of Public Health, nearly one-third of female online daters who were surveyed reported having sex on the first date.[87] She thinks there's already a relationship, but he thinks he just got lucky. In her mind, they've been having this fantastic and meaningful virtual relationship, but in his, it's still only their first date.

## ATTRACTION IN PERSON

I mentioned earlier that the pheromones like copulins that a woman produces when she ovulates can get a man's attention by having the biological effect of raising his testosterone. Imagine a man absent-mindedly standing at a bar when a woman walks by. At that moment the man's buddy elbows him in the side him to get his attention to notice the girl. That buddy is testosterone. When a man's testosterone gets a bump, it tells him, "Hey, look at her!"

So what can a woman do, short of dousing herself in pheromones? She can easily and effortlessly give him a nudge by doing one small thing. What is this magical act? You already know it—the smile.

Remember ladies, you're the *prize*. Therefore, when a woman smiles at a man, it can feel like the slot machine just paid off. The glint of her pearly whites can be saying, "Ding, ding, ding! We have a winner!" And, since he's preprogrammed to pursue, expect him to respond.

This theory was supported in a study that discovered that men tend to overestimate a woman's attraction to them. In fact there may be an evolutionary bias for this. As Carin Perilloux, a researcher at Williams College, explains it: "There are two ways you can make an error as a man. Either you think, 'Oh, wow, that woman's really interested in me'—and it turns out she's not . . . [or] she's interested, and he totally misses out. He misses out on a mating opportunity." So the guys who went for it scored more often and passed on their overperceiving tendencies to their offspring.[88]

When a man perceives a woman as receptive to him, it sends a testosterone-raising jolt right through him. Contrary to the studies that show men tend to be more aggressive when their testosterone shoots up, in this case, they become friendlier—to a woman, that is.

A study conducted in the Netherlands found a direct connection between a man's testosterone bump and his incentive to court. An even more interesting study found that a testosterone spike causes a man to be more caring toward a woman. The researchers elevated the men's testosterone levels in a nonphysical contest. They then placed each participant with either an unfamiliar man or woman. They found that the men with the greatest testosterone increase showed more interest in the woman, engaging in more self-presentation, smiling more, and making more eye contact. In fact, the researchers state that this is the first study that provides direct evidence that elevated testosterone levels increase affiliative behavior (friendly, positive gestures, such a smiling and touching) toward women.[89] In other words, when a guy gets that testosterone nudge, he's automatically programmed to sweet-talk a woman.

## WHEN THE SMILE FAILS

Tina told me the story of meeting Brad through mutual friends. The night they met she flirted, but Brad graciously backed away. Tina later learned, much to her embarrassment, that Brad was married. Brad and his wife were going through a difficult time, and that was why he was at the party without her. Three years later, Tina was out shopping when she heard a man's voice call out her name. It was Brad. Brad and his wife had tried to work it out but decided to divorce. Although Tina had all but forgotten about that night, Brad hadn't. Tina's smile had left an indelible memory. Now that he had been single for a while, he was ready, willing, and able to pick up where they left off that night.

Now you have each other's attention. What do you do next? It's time to determine if this is someone that you would want to risk falling in love with. That's decided in the next phase on the road to falling in love—dating.

# PART II

# DATING

# CHAPTER

# LOVE POTION

Now that you're both attracted, the next big question is: How do you move from attraction to falling in love? This is the question that I initially set out to understand and the one that helped me connect all the pieces of love.

When I first began to ponder this question, I was on vacation visiting my family. My cousin has a PhD in biochemistry. I told him what I had discovered about what happens to you scientifically when you're falling in love (I explain this in detail in Chapter 7). I explained to him that when you fall in love, some neurotransmitters drop while others rise. I also told him how certain parts of our brain shut down. Then I said, "I want to understand how we get there; how do we fall in love? I believe it's a biochemical process." He nodded in agreement. *Excellent*, I thought.

I then said, "I think that certain neurotransmitters may build up and reach a tipping point, and on the other side of that point, we fall in love." Again, he nodded, with a facial expression that said "plausible."

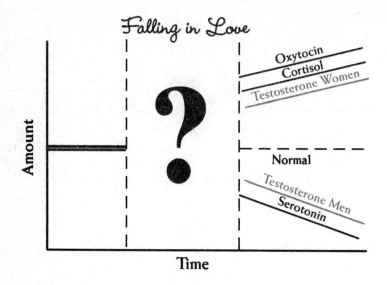

I was getting excited. Hopefully, by talking about it with him, I would get closer to figuring out the mechanism for falling in love. I started to pose my next comment, but before I could continue, my then ninety-five-year-old grandmother, who had been listening intently, spoke up. She said, "You youngsters don't understand anything about falling in love." I was stunned by her comment, but also curious.

So I responded, "I know; that's what I'm trying to figure out, Granny." (We all call her Granny.)

"Your problem is that you young girls jump into bed too quickly. You fall in love, but a boy doesn't fall in love that way." she said.

Surprised, I looked over her shoulder at my cousin. He rolled his eyes as if to say, "You started this."

I decided to hear what she had to say, so I asked, "Okay, Granny, so then how does a boy fall in love?"

"Back in my day, a girl understood that if you wanted a boy to fall in love with you, you couldn't have sex with him right away."

Now I've heard this line of thinking before. In fact, there are many different theories along this line, such as "The Three-Date Rule," which states that you shouldn't have sex until the third date, and "The Ninety-Day Rule" from Steve Harvey's book *Act Like a Lady, Think Like a Man*, where he tells women to wait ninety days before having sex with a man. But the question is, are these biologically plausible or are they just old wives' tales? I looked back at my cousin with raised eyebrows as if to ask, "What do you think?"

His face was no longer saying "plausible." I don't think he was buying the *postpone sex for a man to fall in love* thing.

But since I had heard this before, I decided to ask Granny another question.

"If I want a guy to fall in love with me, Granny, how long should we wait to have sex?"

Her eyes twinkled, "Ah, yes, that really is the question now, isn't it?"

She sat with a smug grin on her face as I waited in anticipation.

Then she said, "The secret to getting a guy to fall in love with you is you wait until he falls in love first."

What? I felt a kick in my chest and a painful ringing in my ears. I felt like I had just climbed the mountain to reach the guru at the top who had the secret to life, but when I finally asked him, all he gave me was a circular riddle.

Over her shoulder, my cousin shook his head again, as if to say, "You asked."

I was already in deep, so I decided to continue and ask one more question.

"Okay, Gran, how do I know when he falls in love?"

"Oh, that's easy," she said. "You know he has fallen in love when he commits."

I looked over at my cousin. He drops his head and just shook "no." Then he spoke up and said, "Okay, Granny, let's take you back home."

It was obvious that my cousin, the brilliant scientist, was not buying into my grandmother's theory. So I returned home defeated but even more determined to figure how we fall in love.

## FALLING IN LOVE

Many scientists believe that falling in love is a neurological process, but understanding the exact mechanism is tricky. To understand the science, experiments must be run.

As you can imagine, doing this type of experiment on people would be difficult. You'd have to get a group of people together that had just fallen in love and ask them to participate, saying something like, "We would like to inject you with a substance in the center of your brain to see what effect it has on your love life. Interested? It pays fifty dollars."

If they said yes, the researchers would have to follow them and make observations, followed by conclusions: "Oh look, he just cheated; it looks like love was successfully blocked." Just finding participants would be tough. Then, imagine the ethical and moral logistics involved.

When experiments have issues like these, we often turn to animal models for study. But what animals fall in love? Helen Fisher separates attraction from love when one person begins to take on special meaning.[89] In most cases, that's when people form couples, rejecting other suitors and choosing to date exclusively

We know of many bird species that tend to mate for life. However, to get close to human physiology, it's best to choose a mammal. The majority of mammals are nonexclusive. Not too many animals live out the vow "until death do us part." Many have harems, while others may mate with one partner but not form pairs like we do.[90]

Researchers found an unlikely model in the monogamous prairie vole (*Microtus ochrogaster*). Scientists found that once a prairie vole has mated for more than fourteen hours, both males and females will show a preference, choosing their partner over a new companion.[91] Because they form exclusive bonds, these little creatures have given us valuable clues as to what happens to us when we fall in love.

## WHAT WE LEARNED FROM THE VOLES

Scientists suspected for a long time that love involved neurotransmitters that were linked to sexual attraction and partner selection. The problem was, which neurotransmitters and how do you prove it? One of the first neurotransmitters researchers looked at was dopamine. This makes sense, because dopamine is a chemical released by the reward center of the brain. The pleasurable feelings produced by dopamine cause an individual to want to repeat the behavior that triggered its release.

Dopamine is critical to motivation and the pursuing of rewards. Some researchers believe its principal role is to signal the brain to seek something enjoyable. It's released during gratifying experiences, such as taking drugs, smoking, eating, and having sex.[92] Dopamine keeps us coming back to the things we love for more.

Researchers at Emory University found that when a female prairie vole mates with a male prairie vole, her dopamine increases by 51 percent. The researchers also found that mating caused an increase in dopamine in males.[93] Of course, an increase in a substance doesn't mean the substance caused the reaction, which in this case was bonding. To make sure that it was dopamine that was causing the attachment between the voles, the researchers then injected the voles with a substance that blocked the effect of dopamine to see what happened. When the dopamine was blocked, the lovebirds broke up. The researchers found that the dopamine antagonist blocked the mating-induced partner preference.[94] After this study, it appeared that dopamine might be nature's love potion.

However, this needed to be confirmed. The Emory team decided to run one final test. To make sure it was dopamine and not some other neurotransmitter that might've been produced by mating, they took several unpaired voles that had not mated and injected them with a substance that increased dopamine. If the voles then showed a partner preference without mating, but only by having an elevated dopamine, level this would confirm that dopamine caused the bonding.

I can only imagine how excited the team was when they came in the next morning to find the little fluffy voles playing house. The researchers had confirmed that dopamine facilitated partner preference without mating in both male and female voles.[95] This was huge! It could mean that causing an increase in someone's dopamine level could make him or her fall in love. So what causes an increase in dopamine?

## THE DOPE ON DOPAMINE

In the 1950s, James Old and Peter Milner of McGill University pioneered a series of experiments that exposed the nature of dopamine to the world. They implanted tiny electrodes into a rat's brain. Then they gave the rat access to a lever. If the rat pressed the lever, it received an electrical pulse. The researchers predicted that the rat would hit the lever once, identify the sensation as pain, and avoid depressing the lever again. But that's not what happened. To the researchers' surprise, the rat seemed to enjoy hitting the lever. In fact, they couldn't coax the rodent away from it. The rat was like some crazed Morse code operator, repeatedly pressing the lever—up to two thousand times per hour.[96] Often, the rat chose to depress the lever rather than eat or drink. Later, scientists discovered that dopamine was being stimulated by the electric impulses. Because of that, for many years, dopamine was considered to be the brain's "pleasure chemical."[97]

Today, dopamine is considered to be much more. It's widely recognized as critical to reward, learning, and addiction. Virtually all drugs of abuse (including heroin and other opiates), alcohol, cocaine, amphetamines, and nicotine activate dopamine. Also, natural rewards, like food, positive social interactions, and even humor, activate dopamine. And, of course, one of my favorites, sweets like sugar and candy cause a rush of dopamine to flood the bloodstream.[98] This may be why some men bring candy to a woman on a first date, or why he gives candy at Valentine's Day. He's hoping to help accelerate her falling in love with him.

So did Aunt Bea really have the key to love? If you want a man to fall in love with you, should you douse him with sugar, bake him a pie, or ply him with cookies? I'm afraid not. While it does appear that dopamine is important in pairing up with someone, there is one problem: although dopamine skyrockets with sexual attraction, scientists have found that it's subject to something called the "Coolidge Effect."

## THE COOLIDGE EFFECT

Legend says that one day President Calvin Coolidge and his wife were touring a chicken farm. Mrs. Coolidge was walking ahead of her husband when she spotted an amorous rooster. Quite taken by the affection the rooster was showing the hen, Mrs. Coolidge inquired of her attendant, "Is he like that all the time?" She pointed at the rooster Romeo.

"Oh, yes, ma'am. Every day," the attendant stated.

Delighted, Mrs. Coolidge said, "Oh, you must show him to President Coolidge."

The attendant ran back as instructed and said to the president, "Sir, your wife wanted me to point out that rooster to you."

The president looked over and noticed the obvious affection the rooster was showing the hen and said, "I see. Is that rooster like that all the time?"

"Oh, yes, sir. All day, every day, sir."

"I see. Let me ask you another question."

"Of course, sir," said the attendant.

"Tell me, son, is it the same old hen every day?" the president asked.

"Oh, no, sir, it's a different hen every time."

"That's what I thought, son. Now run back and tell Mrs. Coolidge that."

What President Coolidge noted was a phenomenon that's regularly observed in the laboratory and has since been dubbed the Coolidge Effect. This activity was first observed in rats. In an experiment, scientists placed several sexually receptive females in a cage with one male. Prior to introducing the male, the researchers measured his baseline dopamine levels. After introduction, they discovered that the male's dopamine levels began to rise, even when a screen blocked him from the receptive females. Once the male was given the freedom to mingle with the lady rats, his dopamine levels continued to increase as he mated with each of the females. He coupled up, again and again, to the point of exhaustion, all while maintaining his high dopamine level. Only after he was sexually satiated and slumped in the enclosure's corner did his dopamine levels drop. At this point, he became unresponsive to the advances of the ladies. He remained uninterested, despite the licking enticement of the female rats, who were just getting started.

But just as it looked like our rat Romeo was down for the count, the scientists reignited his interest. No matter how tired he was, or how many times he had already mated, this little rodent love machine sprang back into action every time a new female was thrown into the mix. Even when surrounded by several willing (but been-there-done-that) females, the male rat's dopamine levels remained depressed; however, every time a fresh, novel, flavor-of-the-minute female was introduced, his dopamine level shot up like a Texas gusher.[99]

Therefore, there has to be more than just boosting dopamine that causes someone to choose a partner and fall in love. There is. It's not just the presence of dopamine that causes the bonding. Another study found that activation of the dopamine's receptor causes the bonding.[100] This means that dopamine levels can go up and down with relatively little effect. But when its levels stay high enough for a period of time, the receptors can get activated. It actually appears that the presence of elevated dopamine causes the body to produce the receptors. In the Emory University study, researchers found that after a male vole bonded with a female, he had a significant density of dopamine receptors after a period of time.[101] This means that when the dopamine goes up and stays up, it triggers the body to produce the receptors. It's these receptors that are necessary for bonding.

So, maybe dopamine is nature's love potion? Cue the drumroll, please. Brrrrrum. Sorry, not so fast. Dopamine has a definite role in partner selection and in falling in love, but it's obvious from the Coolidge Effect that it can't just be dopamine. Dopamine can fluctuate too much, which would mean you would be falling in and out of love every couple of hours. And, barring teenagers, this usually doesn't happen. Therefore, they began to suspect that dopamine might have a partner of its own.

## THE PARTNER SELECTION NEUROTRANSMITTER HAS A PARTNER OF ITS OWN

Researchers have known for quite some time that other neurotransmitters are involved in forming bonds. In particular, oxytocin has been called the "love hormone" because it goes up when people are in love, but also because it creates the loving bond between mother and child. Oxytocin is also the reason we love our pets. Just looking at our dogs has been found to increase oxytocin levels.[102]

The Emory University research team decided to test what effects oxytocin had on mating with the voles. Since it's known that oxytocin has an effect on females, they began by infusing the single female rodents. What the researchers found was that the oxytocin injections accelerated females' pair bonding. In fact, now the female vole only required a few moments to be with a male before she bonded with him. But the most surprising part, unlike the earlier test that required mating for her to bond, a single infusion of oxytocin caused her to quickly bond with a male, without sex.[103]

Next, to verify it was the oxytocin and not something else causing the bond, the team injected a chemical to block the effects of oxytocin on already bonded females. They found that when oxytocin was blocked, they lost her partner preference. Combined with the previous dopamine results, this caused the Emory researchers to conclude that dopamine and oxytocin do not work sequentially but rather concurrently. It's the actions of both neurotransmitters together that cause the female vole to bond with the male.[104]

It was beginning to look like dopamine and oxytocin were the magical elixirs of love. But there was one big problem. When a male of any species is around a female he's sexually interested in, his testosterone shoots up. This by itself is not the problem. The problem is that testosterone blocks the effects of oxytocin. This means that bonding might be caused by oxytocin and dopamine in females but not in males.

The Emory University team understood this and began searching for another neurotransmitter that might affect male bonding. They didn't have far to look. Vasopressin is a neurotransmitter found in males that's very similar structurally to oxytocin. The team decided to investigate the effect, if any, that vasopressin had on male mate preference. The researchers measured the level of vasopressin in bonded versus nonbonded males. The team found that bonded males had higher levels of vasopressin. This, of course, by itself didn't tell them much. It could still be something that happened with sex.

Therefore, to test if it was vasopressin that was causing the bonding, they infused the males with vasopressin without mating them to see

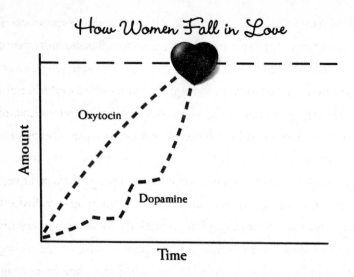

*How Women Fall in Love*

if they still had a partner preference. Sure enough, the males with high levels of vasopressin bonded to a female even without mating with her. To verify the bonding effect of vasopressin, the team then used an antagonist to block the effect of vasopressin on the males. They found that the antagonist prevented pair-bond formation.[105] This confirmed that vasopressin was involved in pair bonding. The conclusion of these studies indicates that oxytocin and dopamine are required for partner selection in females, while vasopressin and dopamine are needed for partner selection in males.

By now you might be thinking, "All these studies are great, but what does this have to do with my love life? I'm not a vole; I'm a human being. What does all of this have to do with me?" Let's take a look.

My first question was, "Is this work with voles applicable to humans?" To find out, I wrote to the lead researcher of one of the studies, Mohamed Kabbaj, a professor of biomedical sciences and neurosciences at the College of Medicine at Florida State University.

I asked him if the social bonding mechanism and/or neurotransmitters are applicable to humans. His response was almost embarrassing. He wrote back, "Of course, Dawn!"[106] Yes, the exclamation point was his. His e-mail included an example of mother and child bonding being highly regulated by oxytocin. I was hoping to get an example about love, but I was beginning to wonder if I would ever get a confirmation.

Fortunately, I found love. Tiffany Love, that is. Tiffany Love, a researcher at the Molecular and Behavioral Neuroscience Institute at the University of Michigan, has thankfully come forth to say that she believes human social bonding mechanisms are linked to neurotransmitters, similar to that of the voles, and that they are engaged in human romantic love.[107] Yahoo!

So the next question is, how do these neurotransmitters cause you to fall in love? One day you're walking along, minding your own business, when you meet someone new. You find this new person attractive. You get a little closer to investigate, and the next thing you know, you fall in love. What happens between the time when you meet and the time when you fall in love?

If you look at the vole studies for a clue, the first thing you'd expect to happen is that your dopamine would rise. And, in fact, that's exactly what we see. Researchers at the Institute of Cognitive Neuroscience at the University of London found that attraction activates the dopamine regions in the reward center of the brain.[108] They also found that the greater the attraction, the greater the reward activation. In fact, if the attraction is not reciprocated, the firing pattern decreases, but if the attraction is mutual, and particularly if it's surprising, watch out—this means game on. That's one of the reasons random, unexpected encounters can be the best thing when it comes to finding love. Your dopamine surges give you a euphoric, intoxicating feeling that makes you crave more.

Next, you would expect your oxytocin levels to increase. And again, that's what scientists have discovered. Researchers in Israel found that oxytocin levels are highest in new lovers—higher than singles and even new parents.[109] That's why the world feels so warm and friendly early in a relationship.

How this works when it comes to love is that each time you have a date, or you talk or think about the other person in a favorable manner, your reward circuit adds a little more oxytocin. Oxytocin is the neurotransmitter of trust. So slowly, as you're getting to know and trust someone, your oxytocin levels increase.

Researchers in Sweden decided to test the effect oxytocin had on women's attitudes toward men. In their study they administered an oxytocin nasal spray to both single women and women in relationships and then measured any changes in their behavior. They discovered that women became friendlier to men. The effect was greatest on single women.[110] In other words, the oxytocin seemed to motivate a woman to get closer to a man. Its effects were highest on single women, because nonsingle women were already close to a man. Oxytocin gives you a feeling of trust and safety. The world no longer feels like a big, scary place; now it feels warm and inviting, and your feelings of anxiety plummet.

To test the theory that oxytocin helps you get closer to another person, researchers at Duke-NUS Graduate Medical School's Cognitive Neuroscience Lab gave participants either oxytocin or a placebo; then the participants were shown video clips of men and women. A day later the participants were shown pictures of men and women and then asked to decide which of the individuals they would like to learn more about and spend time with. The participants displayed an increased preference for people they had been introduced to immediately following the administration of oxytocin.[111]

Oxytocin can be self-amplifying. That is, it produces a type of positive feedback loop. Each time a couple interacts by socializing or looking at each other, holding hands, or touching each other, small bursts of oxytocin are released. Oxytocin levels increase as the couple continues to interact by talking, touching, and cuddling. A phone conversation produces a little gust that causes you to want to go on a date. Then you go on a date and get a little more oxytocin, which makes you want to kiss good night. Then, you kiss good night and get another heaping gob of feel-good.

This amplifying effect causes a couple's oxytocin levels to increase over time. Oh, and I'm not talking a little bit higher—the oxytocin level from being single to being in a new relationship is almost doubled![112] Oxytocin has also been found to increase eye-gazing in couples, which in turn induces the production of dopamine.[113] The two neurotransmitters work together, amplifying each other and intensifying the couple's connection.

Now some may debate which comes first, dopamine or oxytocin? For example, Abigail Marsh, associate professor of psychology at Georgetown University, states: "People who excite romantic feelings in us also probably trigger increases in oxytocin, which results in an increase in dopamine, and then we find that person someone we want to stick with."[114]

At this point, which comes first probably doesn't matter. When it comes to dating, it appears they work in tandem. This would make sense. As you get excited to be with someone, you produce dopamine, which causes you to want to be around him or her, which causes you to produce oxytocin. The more oxytocin you have, the more you want to be around the other person, and if that interaction continues to be positive, you produce more dopamine.

Eventually the two neurotransmitters build up until you reach a tipping point. On the other side of this neurochemical summit is the exciting sensation of falling in love.

## LAUREN'S STORY

This slow buildup of oxytocin is the ideal way to fall in love. However, things don't always work as we expect. Take Lauren's story, for example. Lauren wasn't looking for a relationship and had no intention of falling in love. She had just graduated college and was starting a new job in a new town. Her goal was to meet new friends and have some fun.

She joined a meet-up group for single young professionals in the area. They planned different activities to explore the city and to network. One Friday night, Lauren joined the pizza and bowling meet-up. That's when she met Josh. He was also new to the area and starting a new career. They hit it off immediately. The two were on the same team and ended up winning. Afterward, Josh asked her if she would like to get a drink. She did, and they ended up talking for hours.

Josh texted her on Saturday to say he had a great time and wondered if she had plans that night. They planned their first real date. During the date, Josh said he really liked her, but since he was just settling in, he wasn't sure he was ready for a "full-blown" relationship. Lauren readily agreed, stating she was only looking for something "casual."

That evening they participated in a whiskey-tasting event and then decided to stop by Josh's place. He said that the whiskey had affected him more than he liked and that he'd call an Uber to get her safely home, or if she would like, she was welcome to stay there for the night. Lauren decided to stay. They had a few more drinks, talked, and eventually fell into bed and enjoyed a hot and steamy night. Over the course of the next three weeks, Lauren and Josh hooked up periodically, once even spending the entire weekend together.

Then one evening Lauren was out with a couple of coworkers and spotted Josh. Lauren ran over to say "Hi," but Josh was rather standoffish and distant. Lauren quickly figured out why. Josh was on a date with another woman. Lauren became irate, asking Josh "if he was sleeping with her too?" Lauren stormed out of the restaurant in tears. Why did she have such a response to someone who she herself described as "just casual"? Somewhere over the course of those weeks together, Lauren had fallen in love.

You see, oxytocin builds up slowly as we spend time with someone. But you get a huge surge when you have an orgasm. Because of their sexual relationship, Lauren had quite a few of those. Since she also liked Josh, she was producing dopamine, and because of the sex, she was producing oxytocin. Those two neurotransmitters built up quickly, and she tipped over into love.

But Lauren falling in love was not the big problem here. The real problem here was that Lauren fell in love, while Josh was still just "being casual." That's because men fall in love differently.

## WHY MEN FALL IN LOVE DIFFERENTLY

Recall how I mentioned that testosterone blocks the effect of oxytocin. When a man meets a woman he's interested in, his testosterone goes up. So although his oxytocin may be surging, it doesn't affect him like it affects a woman. A little sex and she's on her way to love. But, in a kind of cruel twist of fate from Mother Nature, a little sex may actually prevent him from falling in love. Allow me to explain.

Taking a lesson from the voles, to find out how a man falls in love, we need to take a look at vasopressin. Fortunately for us, a Swedish team decided to look at the effects of vasopressin on a human's love life. The vole study made it clear that vasopressin was important in pair bonding, so scientists decided to see if a similar effect could be found in people. The team studied 553 couples to determine if vasopressin contributed to the satisfaction of marital (and long-term) partners.

Vasopressin is encoded in men by a particular gene. There are three versions of the gene, a larger version (the gene with two copies), a medium version (the gene with one copy), and a small version (the gene with no copies). The bonding effects are inversely proportional. The larger version of the gene produces vasopressin with the weakest bonding properties. Therefore, the men with two copies of the gene showed a lower partner bonding score (PBS). They also had less partner satisfaction, less affection, more relationship problems, and were less likely to be married or cohabiting.

On the other hand, the men with the small version of the gene had the highest PBS scores, greater partner satisfaction, showed more affection, and were more likely to be married.[115] But for our purposes, the version of the gene is not the important part. The significance here is that these findings indicate that the pair-bonding findings in voles are indeed comparable to humans.

Also, unlike oxytocin, which is blocked by testosterone, a man's vasopressin appears to be enhanced by it. When adult male rodents that were castrated at birth were given vasopressin, they showed no bonding tendency. However, when vasopressin was dispensed to a male that had been castrated as an adult and already had testosterone in his system, he showed some bonding tendencies.

Taken together, these results suggest that there may be a synergistic effect with the combination of dopamine, vasopressin, and testosterone in men that may cause them to fall in love.

### Figure 5. How Men Fall in Love

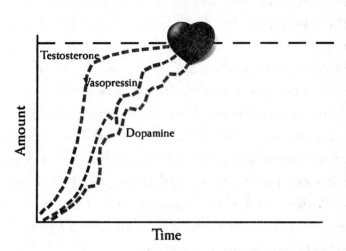

Now at this point, you're probably thinking, "this neurotransmitter stuff is all great, but what does it mean for me?" Now, you know I didn't drag you through all this biological drama just to drop you. Here is the critical part: now that you know which neurotransmitters are involved in the process of falling in love, you hold the magic ticket.

## HOW MEN FALL IN LOVE

If you recall, I began this chapter with a conversation with my cousin and grandmother. Well, it was mostly a conversation with my grandmother, because my cousin just nodded. The point is, by now you can probably guess who was right. The process of falling in love is a biochemical reaction. In women, oxytocin and dopamine build up until the levels reach the tipping point and result in falling in love, while in men testosterone, dopamine, and vasopressin must build up over time until levels reach the tipping point of falling in love

But what about what my grandmother said? Is there any merit in the assertion that sex and/or commitment have any effect on falling in love? For a woman to fall in love, her oxytocin level needs to rise. This happens slowly, as she spends time with a guy. But this is not the only way she gets oxytocin. A woman also gets a huge burst when she has an orgasm. That's right—having sex can cause a woman to fall in love quicker, like my grandmother mentioned.

But what about the other part? What happens if she waits to have sex? Will it cause a man to fall in love? If you recall, one of the main neurotransmitters involved for a man to fall in love is vasopressin. Vasopressin increases in a man when he's sexually excited. However, there's a catch. Although it goes up when he does (mechanically speaking and otherwise), it also goes back down after he does. That is to say, vasopressin becomes elevated when a man is sexually stimulated, such as when he's thinking about sex, but it decreases rapidly after he has an orgasm.

In other words, my grandmother might be on to something. Although I mentioned that the elevation of oxytocin and vasopressin are important for people to fall in love, I left out one more important thing. Researchers at Florida State University discovered that it's not just the amount of the neurotransmitter that's important; you also have to have the receptors for the neurotransmitters.

The formation of the receptors, like the ones I mentioned with dopamine, takes time and the process gets started by the presence of the neurotransmitter. That is to say, your body produces oxytocin or vasopressin, then the presence of the oxytocin sends a message that receptors are needed. Your body then builds the receptors for the neurotransmitters.[116] However, as you can imagine, this process of building new receptors doesn't happen right away.

Therefore, delaying sex with a man causes his vasopressin levels to increase and stay up long enough for the receptors to be built and then filled. Once that happens for a long enough span of time, it can cause him to fall in love. In fact, in one study, researchers found that an increased amount of receptors caused the prairie vole to bond faster even without mating.[117]

But what about the part grandmother said about commitment? Remember, I asked, "How do I know when he falls in love?" She answered, "You know he has fallen in love when he commits." Was she on to something or was this unfounded? For the answer to that, we need to take a look at a study conducted by the U.S. Air Force.

The U.S. Air Force followed 2,100 veterans for more than a decade, giving them a physical exam about every three years. One of the things they measured was the servicemen's testosterone levels. What they discovered was rather remarkable. The study found that the veterans' testosterone levels fluctuated with their marital status. Single servicemen had rather high testosterone, which is not surprising. However, the surprising part was that once a man married, his testosterone level plummeted. Not only that, it stayed low as long as he stayed married. Once he was contemplating divorce, his testosterone level began to rise again. In fact, the researchers found that men's testosterone levels doubled just before and after their breakups. This made their testosterone levels the best predictor of divorce.[118]

Imagine if you tuned in to the *Maury Show* one day and saw women bringing their husbands on. Instead of a paternity test, they ask Maury for a testosterone test, saying, "Maury, I think my husband's thinking about leaving me. Can you test him?" Then we watch as Maury opens his famous manila envelope to announce, "Yes, he's thinking about divorce." Or better yet, "No, he still loves you. Now go home, you two, and have a good time."

The point of these test results is that when a man marries a woman, his testosterone level drops. But at what point does it drop? Does it drop when he marries or when he commits to a woman? To find the answer, researchers at Harvard University decided to run some tests. They had 122 men fill out a relationship questionnaire and provide a saliva sample for testing. The results revealed that men in committed, romantic relationships had 21 percent lower testosterone levels than men not involved in such relationships. Furthermore, the testosterone levels of married men and unmarried men who were involved in committed, romantic relationships did not differ.[119] This suggests that it's not marriage that causes his drop in testosterone but rather the commitment to a monogamous relationship that causes the nosedive.

This, of course, caused my grandmother's statement to come rushing back into my head. "You know he has fallen in love when he commits." Maybe she was really on to something. By holding off on sex, you give vasopressin a chance to build up, but even more significant might be the commitment. When he commits, his testosterone level drops. As I'll explain in more detail in Chapter 7 ("Falling in

Love"), a man's testosterone level drops when he falls in love. This can happen naturally when all three neurotransmitters build up to the tipping point or it can be caused by a commitment. This drop in testosterone is significant for a man to be in love. A higher testosterone level blocks the effects of oxytocin, but with the lower testosterone level, the bonding effects of oxytocin can occur.

Therefore, by delaying sex and asking for a commitment, you're ensuring that he falls in love with you, either by the action of vasopressin or by the action of oxytocin. This supports my grandmother's assertions to wait until you're in a committed relationship to have sex. Once a woman has sex, her oxytocin level skyrockets, causing her to fall in love. Therefore, when you wait and ask for a commitment, it ensures that you both fall in love at the same time. This, of course, confirms something I already knew: Granny is brilliant!

---

## RECAP

For a woman to fall in love, she needs a combination of dopamine and oxytocin.

For a man to fall in love, he needs a combination of dopamine, vasopressin, and testosterone.

**Dopamine:** We get a sudden, short-lived burst of dopamine when we like something, but we build a sustainable level when we work (for men) or if we wait (for women) for something desirable.

**Oxytocin:** Women slowly build up oxytocin when they interact socially and touch and talk with someone they're attracted to. They get a sudden burst when they become sexual. Men, on the other hand, build up oxytocin, but testosterone blocks its effects.

**Vasopressin:** Men increase levels of vasopressin when they get sexually excited, but they quickly lose the level when they ejaculate.

**Testosterone:** A man's testosterone level drops when he commits to a woman, making him more susceptible to the bonding effects of oxytocin. And his levels stay low as long as he's committed.

Now I realize that there is a big gap between meeting someone and asking for a commitment. That gap is the dating process. Fortunately, you can use the knowledge gleaned from this chapter to safely and successfully navigate through the dating process by understanding what effects these rising and falling neurotransmitters have on you and your partner. I'll also explain how and when to ask for that commitment.

# CHAPTER

# DATING WISDOM: WHAT WORKS, WHAT DOESN'T

Now you know what biochemical processes have to happen for someone to fall in love. For women, oxytocin and dopamine build up, and for men, testosterone, dopamine, and vasopressin build up until they reach a tipping point. On the other side is the exhilarating sensation called "falling in love." On paper this seems pretty straightforward: add a little vasopressin, mix in a little dopamine, top off with a splash of testosterone, shake, not stir, and voilà—you have a man in love. Of course, anyone who's been there knows it's not that easy.

It's not just a simple additive process; rather, you have this pesky time period where the neurotransmitters need to build up. It's also the time when we are evaluating the other person. Is this someone we want to risk falling in love with? Is this someone we want to spend the rest of our life with? During this time, any misstep can cause the process to hopelessly derail. What do we call this perilous in-between place where one miscalculation, one wrong word, or a slight body-language hint can send you to the lonely depths of rejection hell? It's called "dating."

Open up any woman's magazine or watch a daytime talk show and you're bombarded with tips and advice when it comes to dating. Go into any bookstore and you'll find a whole section devoted to dating books. Surf the Internet and you'll see banners for dating sites, coaches, and services. It seems like everyone has something to help the lovelorn. But how do you know what is the right thing to do?

Here's the good news. You now hold in your hand the true secret to successful dating. In this chapter, we'll take a closer look at how the brain and the neurotransmitters work on the path to falling in love. Once you understand how things operate, you'll know what to do if your goal is love. You'll understand what advice works, why, and what behaviors help you to get to love. Let's begin by taking a closer look at what's happening in your brain.

## THE REWARD PATHWAY

Not surprisingly, since love is our greatest reward, the process of falling in love begins within the reward pathway. I've briefly made ref-erence to the reward center and pathway already. However, in order to understand what dating advice works and why, we need to take a closer look. The brain's reward pathway is an ancient circuit encom-passing some of the more primitive brain structures. It's believed to have evolved over a billion years ago. In fact, the chief neurotrans-mitter, dopamine, affects the behavior of most creatures, including worms and flies.[120] In humans, this pathway also incorporates our more recently evolved prefrontal cortex, the thinking, planning, and reasoning part of our brain. This allows us a degree of restraint. By adding the prefrontal cortex to the pathway, you now are not completely swayed by your biological urges. You're not running purely on instinct. You have the ability to judge, weigh, and calculate the benefits versus the costs of each decision.

Essentially, when you sense something you want or believe might be nice to have, dopamine is triggered in your brain reward pathway. It starts in your ventral tegmental area (VTA) or reward center, which resides on the floor of your midbrain. Activity in this area is associated with pleasure, general arousal, focused attention, and motivation to pursue and acquire rewards.[121] You walk into a mall and the smell of coffee fills your nose. Your next thought is *Boy, a caramel latte sounds good right now*. Or maybe you see a sign that says "Half-price off all shoes." Or maybe you bump into a friend who has a cute coworker who just happens to be single like you. Whatever the reward might be—coffee, shoes, or the potential of love—they can all trigger your reward pathway by releasing dopamine. You then experience a pleasant feeling that motivates you to want more. Like the rat that kept depressing the lever, you will continue to pursue the desired item as long as it feels good.

It's called a "pathway" because once triggered, a response travels a circuit that includes the amygdala and parts of the frontal cortex, particularly the ventromedial prefrontal cortex, or that part of the brain that makes judgments (hereafter referred to as your "Judge"). Together these structures help to determine if a reward is worth pursuing or doing again or not. If the amygdala and the Judge both say "yes," the activity continues. However, if one or the other says "no," you lose interest. You want that caramel latte, but you want to look good in your new jeans more. Therefore, the cost of that latte in calories outweighs its short-term, tasty benefits.

There are two other important structures along this pathway: the hippocampus and the hypothalamus. The hippocampus, if you recall, is used slightly differently in men than in women. Both use it for memory, but women are better at remembering color and details, while men tend to remember directions. When a woman meets an attractive other, she remembers what he looks like, while a man remembers where a woman is located. He's built to find her again and she's built to remember what he looks like when he returns—just another reminder that men are built to chase and women are built to choose.

When it comes to love, the hypothalamus can also get involved. If the other structures along the reward pathway don't veto the response, it finally gets to the hypothalamus. The hypothalamus is responsible for releasing oxytocin and vasopressin, the neurotransmitters needed to fall in love. All these structures work together to continue the chase or to cause it to come to a halt. When you meet someone you like, your Judge says, "Me likey," the amygdala sounds an alarm to say, "Hey, pay attention," and the hippocampus says, "Let's remember this."

Next, your ventromedial prefrontal cortex, or Judge, is triggered again. Your Judge now begins a careful evaluation. This reminds me of a game I played as a child called "Red Light, Green Light." As the Judge asks questions and gets a "yes," it's a green light, and the response keeps going, but if the answer is "no," it's a red light and everything stops. Often the first question is "Are they single?" Yes, green light. Next, "Are they interested in me?" Yes, green light. "Am I interested in them?" Yes, green light.

If you keep getting green lights, your reward center gushes with dopamine. Your amygdala's alarm buzzes to get your attention, which can make you nervous and anxious. Your hippocampus is triggered to remember and your Judge carefully evaluates, and each time all goes well and the response makes another lap around the circuit, your hypothalamus releases oxytocin or vasopressin, and you slowly waltz your way toward love.

Of course, if it was as easy as it sounds, you wouldn't need so many dating books, advice columns, dating coaches, and relationship therapists. The problem is that each of these parts, including the neurotransmitters, has idiosyncrasies that can enhance or hinder the process. Much of the common relationship advice addresses these issues. Let's look at some of the science behind some popular dating advice.

## BEING RECEPTIVE

I mentioned in Chapter 5 that when a man is attracted, his testosterone gives him a nudge. What happens next can either give him a green light with its first lap around the reward circuit or it can shut the process down. The way a man gets a green light from a woman is when she's receptive.

When we first start dating, each of us is wondering the same thing: *Do I like this person and do they like me?* If you decide you like someone, the next thing that happens is you begin looking for clues that they like you. These are subtle, often subconscious indications that the conversation is tipping into your favor. For a man, when a woman smiles or twists her hair, an electrifying jolt can be sent to his reward center. His insides start jumping around like Rudolph the red-nosed reindeer when he was first kissed, exclaiming, "She likes me, she likes me!"

Since vasopressin is one of the neurotransmitters of love for men and it increases with sexual longing, men are looking for evidence of desire. A man's desire for a woman is important, but it may be much more important for her to desire him. Men can be attracted to a myriad of woman, but when one reciprocates interest, it can be surprisingly intoxicating.

In my workshops, one question I often get is "How can I let a man know I'm interested?" Since I advise women to let him chase, they want to know how to get his attention without pursuing. I tell them the biggest thing a woman can do is smile. Now, I'm not talking about a quick smile followed by putting your head down. Many women make the mistake of cutting off the smile too soon. I usually demonstrate the "I like you smile" by looking at a man, smiling, then letting my eyes drift up and down him, coming back to meet his eyes. Then, almost as if I'm embarrassed to show such a display, I turn away demurely. This brief, three-second encounter sends a message straight to his reward center that says, "Stop whatever you're doing and get over there!" It also starts flooding his bloodstream with super-charged testosterone, so he's now ready to start the chase.

You can signal desire during dates by tilting your head or subtly touching your lips, or, better yet, by touching your date. A brush of his arm or a pat on his hand sends a message that you would enjoy more contact with him. Because women fall in love with a buildup of dopamine and oxytocin, men are looking for evidence of that. Oxytocin is the cuddle hormone, so those slight touches can indicate that oxytocin has entered the building. And, as a woman's oxytocin builds up, she begins to trust him.

As you go out on dates and get to know each other, he's looking for signs that you're enjoying being with him and that you trust him more and more. When you smile, make eye contact, and lean toward him, it sends a nonverbal message to him that you like him and trust him.

The entire process of dating is a slow lowering of defenses and becoming more vulnerable by building trust. Often your first date is a meeting in a neutral location. Then if you like him and trust him, you demonstrate vulnerability by allowing him to pick you up on the next date. As your trust for him grows, maybe you'll invite him in. You now trust him enough to be alone with him. The more you show you're building trust, the more enticing you are to him.

This is why the damsel in distress is such an alluring figure. If a man can swoop in and save a woman, help her carry a heavy package, change a tire, or rescue her from the villain who tied her to the train tracks, she'll instantly trust him. He's done a week's worth of work in a few short minutes.

This is also why a sense of humor is often the number 1 desired personality trait women want in a man.[122] Humor helps lower your defenses. You tend to trust people more when they make you laugh. But there is another important reason that humor is so important: it triggers the reward pathway.[123] Humor can give your reward pathway a bunch of green lights.

## YOU NEED TO LOVE YOURSELF BEFORE YOU CAN LOVE ANYONE ELSE

Dating is scary for everyone. Men and women both crave and fear love. You want love, but in order for someone to get close to you,

you have to become vulnerable. That vulnerability is terrifying. In fact, some people simply take themselves out of the dating market. They work too much, or convince themselves that there is no one "out there" for them.

Those who are brave enough to venture into the open waters of dating discover that the waters can be choppy. Dating is rife with uncertainty. Because of this, it's normal to experience high levels of anxiety, which is caused by triggering of the amygdala.

This apprehension and uncertainty can make you feel uncomfortable and fill your head with thoughts of doubt. *Does he like me? Will he call? Is he a good choice? Will he make a good father? Does he want children? Do I want children? Will he still like me if I don't want children?* Because you have so many judgments and decisions to make, the neural activity along the reward loop can become intense. Sometimes this anxiety can cause a woman to make poor choices, just to quell the angst. This was Cheyenne's pattern.

## CHEYENNE

Cheyenne is a petite brunette in her late twenties. She's smart and attractive, so to look at her, you'd think dating would be easy for her. But Cheyenne doesn't like dating. In fact, she feels like she's not any good at picking men.

Her last three relationships were horrible. The first one turned out to be a drug addict. The second one had a porn addiction, and the third ran off with her now–ex–best friend. By the time she had met me, she had all but given up on dating.

Cheyenne's problem was not necessarily the men she picked. Her problem was her amygdala. When she met a guy she was interested in, she'd immediately become nervous; the anxiety that dating caused was almost unbearable. She'd find herself checking her phone every five minutes, Googling his name, and stalking his Facebook and Instagram accounts.

If he called for a date, it almost made it worse. Now she had to worry about what to wear, getting her nails done, how she should wear her hair and makeup, and what she should say on the date. During the date she found herself listening to every word he said, looking for clues. *Is he a cheater? Does he really want a relationship? Will he hurt me?* Her internal dialogue became so loud that she missed things that he said.

Then came the pressure for sex. Cheyenne said she went by the "three-date" rule, where she waited to have sex until the third date. But she admitted that the tension and pressure would become so great, she sometimes caved on the first date. She said she just wanted to "get it over with." When I pressed her about what she was getting over with, she said, "Once we had sex, it just seemed easier." It turned out what Cheyenne experienced was the pacifying of her amygdala.

In a way Cheyenne was playing a game of Russian roulette. When she had sex, her oxytocin surge quieted her amygdala, diminishing her anxiety substantially, which made her feel better. This seemed like a great fix, but it wasn't. The problem was that her oxytocin levels were high, which diminished her ability to judge her date.

In a joint study by the University of Zurich and Claremont Graduate University in California, researchers looked at the effects of oxytocin on trust. They found that intranasal administration of oxytocin increased trust among people, but it was a unique type of trust. They found that oxytocin specifically affected an individual's willingness to accept social risk arising through interpersonal interactions.[124]

In other words, oxytocin helps you get past your natural defenses and interact in a deeper way. In fact, researchers found that when subjects were given nasally administered oxytocin, they displayed "the highest level of trust" twice as often as a control group.[125]

Oxytocin produces feelings of instant connection and believability, which clouds reality. Therefore, when Cheyenne slept with a man, her rush of oxytocin erased any doubts she had about him. He was instantly believed and trusted.

To top it off, all Cheyenne needed was to be excited about seeing him, which increased her dopamine and set her up to fall in love. The problem was that falling in love so early in the relationship shut down the parts of Cheyenne's brain she needed to determine if he was a good fit for her or not.

The signs might be there. You see him surfing porn sites, notice that he drinks a lot, or see his eyes looking at everyone else but you, but because you have now muzzled your amygdala, it doesn't feel like anything you should worry about. Of course, later his true character becomes too great to ignore—but by then, you're already in a relationship, so the realization is painful.

Cheyenne needed to stop the deleterious relationship pattern she had developed. She would meet a man, get nervous, jump into bed with him to quell her nerves, fall in love, and then realize that he wasn't the right man for her. Her heart would be broken, or worse, she'd spend years trying to "fix" him. She continued this painful pattern for more than a decade.

For her, loving herself was realizing her pattern and making changes to fit her real desires. She wanted a loving relationship with a great guy, but she just couldn't figure out how to get it. Cheyenne had always been plagued with anxiety. She had an overly sensitive amygdala. The larger or more sensitive a person's amygdala, the more anxiety they feel. Individuals who have had trauma, loss, or dysfunction in childhood tend to have larger amygdalae.

Cheyenne's father was an alcoholic. Most of the time he was a sweet and loving father. But then came the nights he would drink. Bedtime became a source of terror for her. When she went to bed, she didn't know if she would sleep through the night or wake up to screaming and fighting. Cheyenne never brought friends home, in case her father showed up drunk. Because of the potential dangers, her amygdala grew larger and more active. Cheyenne became hyper-vigilant. When her father showed up drunk, she needed to get out of the way.

Because of her past trauma, Cheyenne's amygdala turned into the Incredible Hulk whenever she started dating someone. The anxiety made her look for certainty and control, but in the beginning of a relationship, ambiguity is high. Unfortunately, this uncertainty can cause an increase in dopamine. Cheyenne had high anxiety and high dopamine, so all she needed was a big dose of oxytocin, which she got by jumping into bed—then bam! She was in love. Her falling in love temporarily quieted her amygdala. But it also shut down other parts of her brain that she really needed in order to discern if a man was right for her.

What is a better way to handle this type of situation? The answer in this case is what the experts refer to as self-love. Cheyenne needed to love herself first, which involved becoming comfortable with herself. She needed to become aware of her patterns and decide to make changes. Next, she needed to create the list I suggested in Chapter 4 about the must-haves and the deal-breakers. She needed to get clear about what she wanted before she started to date. This would help decrease her uncertainty and allow her dopamine to rise at a more reasonable rate.

Next, Cheyenne needed to deal with her anxiety. Research shows that things like journaling and spiritual practices, such as prayer and meditation, can reduce anxiety and make dating more enjoyable. It may seem strange to see a discussion of spiritual practices in a science-based book. However, researchers at the Harvard-affiliated McLean Hospital have found that those who believe in a benevolent God tend to worry less and be more tolerant of life's uncertainties than those who believe in an indifferent or punishing God.[126] Therefore, developing a connection to a loving God can be an antidote to anxiety.

Another important practice for Cheyenne was meditation. Meditation has been found to shrink the size the amygdala. In a study at Massachusetts University, researchers found that just eight weeks of meditation can reduce the size of the amygdala.[127] A smaller amygdala can help alleviate angst. So now, instead of a crazy Hulk, Cheyenne's amygdala is something akin to a pesky minion. Meditation, even a few minutes a day, is a great way to notice negative belief patterns and become more content. With meditation, journaling, and spiritual practice, Cheyenne is now ready to date in a better way.

There is still a ton of dating advice out there to choose from. Let's take a look at what's next.

## WHEN WOMEN CHASE

Now, let's imagine that a beautiful woman walks into a gathering and spots an attractive man. She decides that she's a modern woman with a degree and a high-power position in her company. There is no reason why she can't walk up and introduce herself to this man. She takes her prefrontal cortex full of accomplishments and women's history and sashays over to him, smiles, and says, "Hi, I'm Jennifer."

At that very second, the man's thought patterns come to a screeching halt. His insides feel like a volcano has just erupted as his testosterone explodes. His amygdala is sensitive to testosterone. Therefore, when his testosterone increases, so does his amygdala activity. At the same time, this deluge of testosterone causes a reduced coupling of his amygdala and the primitive parts of his brain from the reasoning part of his prefrontal cortex.[128] This means that the thinking part of his brain is less connected. The primitive part of his brain says to his prefrontal cortex, "Wahoo, there is a woman here and she's interested in us. I don't want you screwing this up, mister, so I'll be taking over from here." In a way, this leaves him at the mercy of his primitive brain.

As he looks at Jennifer, he becomes electrified with norepinephrine, testosterone, and dopamine. The norepinephrine causes him to get excited. The dopamine triggers the reward center in his brain, and he starts focusing on ways to win Jennifer. His increased testosterone causes him to feel more sexually aggressive. However, because of the weakening of the prefrontal cortex connection, the primitive amygdala is now running the show.

Therefore, as Jennifer is standing there smiling at him, a part of his brain begins to have doubts. Society and culture may have changed rapidly in the last hundred years, but this primitive structure is still old school. In addition, the part of his brain that should be telling him that it's okay for Jennifer to behave this way is not fully connected with the rest of his brain. It may be speaking, but the doubts shout louder.

Recent changes in society and technology have little effect on this because our brains have been shaped by millions of years of evolution. The times may have changed, but our brains are much slower to adapt, particularly the parts concerned with survival and reproduction. Therefore, as Jennifer steps into her rightful place in society, she could inadvertently be triggering ancient, primitive, protective mechanisms in him known as the "opossum effect."

## OPOSSUM EFFECT

The opossum is a black-and-white scavenging omnivorous marsupial. It's the only pouched animal still found in North America. The opossum has endured so long because it possesses a unique survival skill: instead of running away or fighting, it has a switch in its nervous system that causes it to freeze and faint when faced with fear.

This may seem counterintuitive. If the opossum falls down, why doesn't the predator just eat it? The reason this tactic works is because the predator's amygdala sets off an alarm signal in its brain, causing it to back off. It's as if it says, "Hey, chief, this is too easy . . . something's wrong . . . it's not safe . . . let's get out of here!" The opossum's fainting reaction triggers a fight-or-flight response in the predator, causing him or her to become apprehensive about this "too good to be true" meal. According to evolutionists, this tactical response was evolved millions of years ago. It apparently continues to work well, since this little white-faced marsupial is one of the few animals still around that walked with the dinosaurs.

When a woman starts pursuing a man, a similar reaction can happen. When she makes it clear to him that she's intensely interested in him, it can be analogous to her falling down on the floor in front of him. A part of him may be interested, but another part has its doubts. The man's amygdala says, "Hey, chief, that's too easy . . . something's wrong . . . it's not safe . . . let's get out of here!" The man suddenly remembers he left the stove on at home and he's gone.

To test this resistance to something that's "too good to be true" theory, researchers at Dartmouth College conducted an experiment using rhesus monkeys. They showed the monkey food (either a pellet or a marshmallow). Then they gave the monkey one of the items. A food pellet is good when you're hungry, but boring. On the other hand, the marshmallow is considered a yummy treat and enjoyed anytime.

When the scientists showed the monkey a pellet, then gave it to him, his reaction time was quick to accept and eat the pellet. But when they showed him a marshmallow (the prize) but then handed him a pellet, his reaction time slowed. His body language showed that he was apprehensive and disappointed, but eventually he accepted the pellet.

Next, they ran the experiment again, but this time they showed him a pellet and gave him a marshmallow. Since the marshmallow was considered such a treat, you'd expect him to snatch it up quickly. But what they found was the opposite: when presented with a pellet but then given the prized marshmallow instead, his reaction time was even slower than before. In addition to the hesitation, he also looked away from the food, as if to double-check his surroundings. His amygdala just sounded the alarm. The monkey would finally accept the marshmallow, but his reaction time in accepting the unexpected prize was more than twice as long.[129] This experiment shows that it's an innate behavioral response to be leery of something that's "too good to be true." It's something that's prewired into our brains.

Like the monkey, the man may accept the prize. In other words, Jennifer may actually get her man, but it may not be the happy time she was hoping for. He may remain skeptical, never fully believing he hit the romantic jackpot. Without that belief and excitement, he may not build up enough dopamine to fall in love.

Remember, for him to fall in love, he needs a buildup of dopamine, vasopressin, and testosterone. To get the testosterone, he needs the chase.

> *Without the chase, a man may not be able to build up*
> *the neurotransmitters to fall in love.*

## MEN CHASE

By now you're probably wondering why I keep reiterating the phrase "men chase, women choose." I mention it again because many other dating books recommend this, including the classic 1995, no. 1 *New York Times* bestseller *The Rules: The Time-Tested Secrets for Capturing the Heart of Mr. Right*, by Ellen Fein and Sherrie Schneider. Many of the thirty-five rules contained in the book are about letting the man chase, such as: Rule 2: Don't Talk to a Man First (and Don't Ask Him to Dance); Rule 5: Don't Call Him; and Rule 17: Let Him Take the Lead. Fein and Schneider admitted that they didn't understand why this worked, but now that I've explained how the neurotransmitters work, it's time to revisit this concept and show you why.

When a man meets a woman he's interested in, his testosterone surges. This triggers the hypothalamus. The hypothalamus has the very important, sexually dimorphic nucleus of the medial preoptic area also known as "the pursuit spot." Remember it? It's the part of the brain that motivates a man to pursue a woman. This outpouring of testosterone kick-starts his pursuit spot into high gear, which makes him better equipped to pursue than a woman is. But his testosterone may quickly drop if he doesn't chase.

Researchers at the University of Missouri–Columbia found that testosterone levels spike in a man during a challenge. In fact, scientists observed that testosterone levels rose during and after competition if the man won, but diminished following a defeat.[130] Therefore, winning the attention of a woman gives a man a nice testosterone surge.

Anthropologists studying the Tsimané men, a group of forager-farmers in central Bolivia, believe this testosterone spike is an evolutionary adaptation that is critical for survival. While measuring testosterone levels of the Tsimané men, scientists discovered that a physical act such as cutting down a tree resulted in a greater increase in testosterone than directly participating in a competitive sport such as soccer. Testosterone levels are closely related to the availability of food energy. When young men skip even a single meal, their testosterone levels can drop as much as 10 percent. If they fast for a couple of days, their testosterone decreases to castration levels.

However, an acute spike of testosterone increases muscles' ability to take in blood sugar, which in turn enhances performance and reaction times. Therefore, this spike could make the difference between surviving or not. As the researchers noted, "One of the important take-home messages of this study is that if you lose the ability to have the acute spikes in testosterone that increase your ability to chop down trees—chop longer and chop harder—that would be detrimental to feeding your family."[131] In other words, this testosterone spike appears to be an evolutionarily adaptation that's crucial for a man's survival. When he feels it, he feels like a super winner.

However, the University of Missouri–Columbia study also found that when men competed against their friends, their testosterone levels did not change in response to victory or defeat.[132] That is to say, it was not the challenge itself but the way the man interpreted the challenge that changed his testosterone levels. A victory against a friend is not considered a triumph and doesn't produce that celebrated testosterone spike. In the same way, when the mating dance is not considered a challenge, such as when a woman gives in quickly, a victory may not be considered a triumph. Even though he scored a prize, this too easy "non-victory" can leave him still desirous of the hormonal boost and leave him feeling as though something's missing.

## WINNING THE PRIZE

Although Fein and Schneider didn't understand the science behind the rules given in their book, it's interesting that they chose "Be a Creature Unlike Any Other" for Rule No. 1. Wolfram Schultz, professor of neuroscience at the University of Cambridge, has found that novelty enhances dopamine response. Remember, dating is all about the reward pathway.

An unpredicted reward, particularly one that's better than expected, induces dopamine even more.[133] In fact, Schultz believes it can induce three to four times more dopamine, and that might even be a conservative estimate.[134] Therefore, if you're unique in a fun and exciting way, you will cause him to get a nice dopamine boost. Dopamine is important for helping to get past some of the reservations that naturally occur during the early stages of attraction and dating.

In order to keep the dopamine flowing, a man must believe that the ultimate prize is worth the risk. To test the association between dopamine and risk/reward, scientists in London conducted a unique study. Participants were divided into three groups. One group was given levodopa, a drug that increases dopamine levels in the brain. Another took haloperidol, a dopamine receptor blocker. The third was given a placebo. Researchers showed each group symbols associated with winning or losing different amounts of money. To "win" more money, participants had to learn which symbols resulted in which outcomes through trial and error.

The study found that those who took levodopa were 95 percent more likely to choose symbols associated with higher monetary gains than those who took haloperidol (the dopamine blocker). As a result, the levodopa group won more money, but it also lost more money. "The results show dopamine drives us to get what we want, but not to avoid what we fear," said the author of the study, Mathias Pessiglione.[135] In other words, when dopamine is surging through our veins, we become more motivated to take greater risks. Not only does the desire for the reward increase, our fear of loss decreases. Although the group with the higher amounts of dopamine experienced more rewards, they were also disappointed more often, thus not necessarily making out any better than the more cautious group. When we are "doped-up" on dopamine, we are willing to take greater and greater chances for what we perceive as larger prizes. Our brains tell us we can't lose.

The greater the prize, the greater the dopamine and the greater the risk we're willing to take. Conversely, if you have doubts about the value of the prize, you produce less dopamine and are less likely to take a risk. That's why I call a Date: Designating A Time to Evaluate. Each person must decide for him or herself if the reward is worth the risks.

Therefore, for Jennifer to be perceived as the amazing prize she is, she needs to let the man take a few risks to win her. These incremental risks and slow buildup of dopamine are critical for him to fall in love. And when he feels like he won during each task, it gives him that needed boost of testosterone.

Dopamine increases with uncertainty. In her book *Daring Greatly*, Brené Brown describes vulnerability as uncertainty, risk, and emotional exposure, but she also describes it as the birthplace of love. As you become increasingly more vulnerable while dating, the uncertainty increases, causing more dopamine to be released.

> *Dating is about incremental increases in vulnerability.*
> *A Date: Designating A Time to Evaluate.*

## I TOTALLY DISAGREE

A few years ago during a nationwide teleconference, I introduced the concept that a man should chase a woman instead of vice versa. As I was explaining the reasons why I believed that a man should make the first move in the courtship process, the male host interrupted me. He said, "I totally disagree with that. I would love for a woman to come up and talk to me. It would make me feel great, and I would probably go out with her."

After that pronouncement, I began to second-guess this line of thinking and decided to investigate it further. Everything I found pointed back to the concept that men should do the chasing. I kept searching for evidence to support his assertion, but before I could, something else happened: I ran into that host again a few months later at an expo.

"How's the dating going?" I asked.

"Great," he said, flashing his ring finger with the wedding band.

"Wait!" I exclaimed. I was in shock. I asked, "You met someone and got married in the last few months since our teleseminar?"

He laughed and said, "No, I got back together with my wife."

That's when his statement on the teleseminar made sense. He was separated, not divorced, and not really available for a relationship because he obviously wasn't finished with his marriage. However, while he was separated, he would gladly take advantage of an "easy pickings" opportunity if it presented itself. In other words, if a woman walked up to him, he would date her and probably sleep with her if given the chance, but he was not willing to put much effort into it.

The lack of willingness to invest time and energy is an indication that he was not that interested. He was not willing to take any risks, and he was not willing to be vulnerable. He was willing to go for a quick shot of dopamine with the casual encounter and even enjoy a little Coolidge Effect if possible. But he was not willing to risk doing any work that could result in him building up the necessary level of dopamine to fall in love with a new person. That could affect the love he still had for his wife.

> *When a guy is not willing to put forth the effort to pursue a woman, it means he's not willing to risk falling in love.*

Therefore, if you're looking for love, you want the man to pursue. When you make it easy, you might win him for the moment, but if you want him for the long haul, taking the lead may not be the best course of action. In addition to usurping dopamine, you might be triggering the subconscious fear of cuckoldry.

## CUCKOLDRY

Cuckoldry is the fear of investing in offspring that are not genetically yours because of a cheating female. It's a predominant fear of most males in nature. The word "cuckoldry" comes from the cuckoo, a Jamaican parasitic bird. Instead of building its own nest, laying eggs, incubating them, and caring for the hatchlings, the cuckoo simply lays her eggs in another bird's nest and flies away. The poor parasitized bird now expends its time and resources—often to the detriment of its own offspring—to raise another bird's brood.

Biologically speaking, this is the ultimate crime. The unfortunate, innocent bird is participating in its own potential extinction. Therefore, the fear of cuckoldry, or the fear of raising someone else's offspring to the detriment of your own, is a major concern for species that have internal fertilization. In other words, where there is any potential doubt of paternity, the fear of cuckoldry is prevalent.

Surprisingly, the fear of cuckoldry is prevalent even in nonmonogamous species that don't have any expectation of fidelity. The main risk is that the male will lose his reproductive investment—the time in courtship, the nest he built, or the food and care he provided. As with other fears of this type, it's not in the realm of consciousness. He's just wired this way.

If the fear of cuckoldry is provoked in a man, he usually can't articulate what he's feeling. Often he'll simply say something like, "I just didn't feel it with her," or "I don't know, there was just something about her that rubbed me the wrong way." Something caused him to feel he couldn't trust her. Something about her triggered his amygdala to sound the alarm and make a retreat, or at least not a commitment. In other words, some men might not leave physically, just emotionally. He may not pass up the chance at sex, but he'll pass on commitment.

This is the main reason that relationship experts warn you against talking about your exes on your dates. You can tell someone if you've been married before, but leave the gory details for a trusted friend. Unfortunately, the more we like a person, the more tempting it is to reveal it all as a way to expedite intimacy. This tactic can often backfire, eliciting a lot fear quickly and making the pursuit of the relationship too risky.

This is what happened to Paula. She had several first dates but never seemed to get a call back for a second. When we talked about the dates, the reason why the men never called again became quite evident. Paula and her ex were still fighting over the home they own jointly. Although she was the only one living in the house, her ex was there almost on a daily basis. Paula was still wrapped up in the drama of her old relationship, which she freely shared on her dates. She didn't realize it, but her preoccupation with her old relationship sent a subtle message that she wasn't ready or believable enough for a new one.

The good news about the fear of cuckoldry is that it can actually be a good thing. The fear of cuckoldry produces innate behaviors referred to as "mate guarding." In nature, mate guarding is performed by a male to prevent a female from being with another male.

An increase in vasopressin has been linked to aggression toward other males.[136] Protectiveness, possessiveness, and jealousy are all hallmarks of mate guarding. When mate guarding shows up, it can indicate a key turning point in a relationship. As Helen Fisher states, "Humans can feel and express sexual desire towards individuals for whom they feel no romantic attraction, but mate guarding is characteristic of romantic love."[137]

When mate-guarding behaviors happen, it can mean that a person has now taken on special meaning. In other words, when a man starts showing mate-guarding activities toward a woman, it means the relationship is officially no longer just sexual but is moving toward love.

## ON GUARD

In nature, mate-guarding schemes can range from the simple to the downright disturbing. For example, if your concern is that another male may sneak in and have sex with your partner when you're not looking, the best way to handle this may be to just keep having sex. That's what a few amphibians do. Some species of frogs have individual sessions of mating that last for several months. This might not sound like such a big deal, but if you convert the frog's time frame into a percentage of human life, then you get the real picture. The frog's lovemaking would be like having a nonstop sex session that lasted almost ten years.[138] That gives a whole new meaning to the phrase "long-term commitment," doesn't it? "Hey fellas, I got a new girlfriend, I'll see you next decade."

But probably the most innovative, and at the same time unsettling, species is the black widow spider. Many people are aware that the male black widow risks being eaten by the female after mating. But few people realize that the male is really the one who gets the last (kind-of-creepy) laugh. Since he's risking his life to pass on his genes, he makes sure that only his offspring will benefit. Therefore, after sex, he snaps off his own penis inside the female's body, ensuring that she can't mate with any other males.[139] I believe this may be a little extreme.

Scientists believe that the fear of cuckoldry and the subsequent mate-guarding tactics are universal and instinctual. They are so ingrained that biologists have even referred to some of them as irrational or unfounded. For example, scientists at the University of Liverpool were studying fruit flies. In this particular type of fruit fly, the female only mates once. The male doesn't have to participate in mate guarding because he knows that the female will be fertilized with his sperm only. Yet researchers still found mate-guarding behavior in the males. In an experiment, scientists placed males in the area of mating couples. When they placed another male in the vicinity, the first male would increase his mating time with the female by 93 percent, even though the risk of the female being fertilized by another male was remote.[140]

The innate behavior to mate guard can give a man that extra impetus to move past his natural resistance and take the relationship to the next level. After sharing a yachting adventure with a man named Ed, I wasn't sure if I was going to hear from him again. I wasn't sure if he was ready for a committed relationship, and I had to accept that. I was dating some other men at the time, but I was starting to like Ed the best.

A few days after our trip, he called for another date. We had a few more dates and he made it obvious that he would like to become sexual, but he remained respectful. A few times, when my resistance was becoming weak, I had to reiterate my previous statement about wanting a mutually exclusive relationship before we became sexual.

I think I did this more for myself than for his. I was very attracted to him, and standing by my resolve was becoming tough.

Then one night after we had gone out to dinner, Ed came into my apartment. We had a fun night, laughing and talking, but it was getting late. As he got up to leave, my phone chirped, indicating that I had a text message. I casually picked up the phone and glanced at the message. That's when Ed said, "Hey, is that a text message from some *guy* saying good night?"

I tried to act casual, but the red flush of embarrassment on my cheeks gave me away. I didn't say anything, nor did I have to. It was perfectly acceptable for someone to be saying good night to me because I was not in a committed relationship with anyone . . . yet.

Ed was on his way to love; his vasopressin levels were increasing, kicking in his mate-guarding behaviors. Therefore, when Ed believed another guy might be interloping on his prize, it may have motivated him to make a swifter decision. It didn't take long after that for Ed to ask me for exclusivity. By asking me to date him singularly, it shut the good-night texting guy down.

When mate guarding shows up, it's an indicator that he's beginning to become invested. The relationship is taking on more meaning to him. However, if you don't see any of this type of behavior, and especially if he's not willing to chase, it could mean he's just not that into you.

## HE'S JUST NOT THAT INTO YOU

*He's Just Not That into You: The No-Excuses Truth to Understanding Guys,* the 2004 number 1 *New York Times* bestseller, was written by comedian Greg Behrendt and writer Liz Tuccillo. I met Behrendt when he performed at the Fort Lauderdale Improv at the Hard Rock. He explained during his act that he had no intentions of becoming a "relationship guru." He joked that he simply understood men. He knew that if a man was interested in you, he would move a mountain to get to you, so if he wasn't willing to pick up a twenty-ounce telephone, chances were pretty good that "he's just not that into you."

Behrendt's caustic logic rips through any illusions like a rusty chainsaw tearing through a cheap romance paperback. With comments such as, "the word 'busy' is a load of crap and is most often used by assholes," and "a man would rather be trampled by elephants that are on fire than tell you that he's just not that into you." [141] In other words, if a man is interested in being in a long-term, monogamous relationship with you, he'll come after you. But if he's not interested in a long-term monogamous relationship, he's never going to tell you.

The wisdom in this book is that men are not mysterious. The simple truth is that men like to chase you. As the book says, "I know it's an infuriating concept—that men like to chase and you have to let us chase you." [142] If he's not regularly calling, asking you out, dating, wooing, and seeing you, he's not chasing you. He may be calling and seeing you sporadically, or texting at 10:00 PM to pop in for the evening, but that's not chasing.

The most difficult and heartbreaking aspect of this realization is that although your relationship may have started out in full chase, at any point along the way, it can veer off course. Then it's up to the woman to resist the temptation to lower her standards of a loving relationship and subject herself to behavior she finds painful and/or unacceptable. No man is going to grab you by the shoulders and say, "I'm sorry, but I'm really not interested in falling in love with you, but I'd like to have sex with you." Or maybe he would.

The boy band One Direction recently put out a song titled *Perfect*. The song basically tells women, "I'm not going to bring you flowers, take you home to my mother, or be there for you. But if you'd like to have a secret little rendezvous in a hotel room, then I'm your guy." So I guess there are a few men out there who are honest.

Before you become too upset, it's not really his fault. The truth is he's built that way. Falling in love weakens a man, but sex doesn't. Therefore, he's likely to take advantage of a low-risk sexual encounter.

To test the theory that men are more likely to take advantage of a low-risk sexual opportunity, Dr. Russell Clark at Florida State University and Dr. Elaine Hatfield at the University of Hawaii joined together to conduct a study. They had both male and female students go on campus and ask students of the opposite sex one question. The question was "Would you go out with me tonight?" The results showed that 50 percent of the men said "yes" and 50 percent of the men said "no." The women's results were the same, with 50 percent saying "yes" and 50 percent responding "no."

They then decided to do a follow-up question. Again, they had both men and women go on campus and ask the opposite sex a question, but this time they changed the question slightly. Now instead of "Would you go out with me tonight?," they asked "Would you have sex with me tonight?" This slight change in the question resulted in a dramatic change in the answers. In the results of this new round, 100 percent of the women responded "no," which was not surprising. However, now only 25 percent of the men responded "no." That is to say, a whopping majority of 75 percent of the men said, "Yes, I'll have sex with you tonight." In fact, several men responded with "Why do we have to wait until tonight?"[143] This means that given the chance, 25 percent of the men who wouldn't put forth the effort to go out with a woman would have sex with her if given the opportunity. When a man is presented with a chance for easy, low-effort sex, it appears that the majority will try and take it—sometimes immediately.

For men, casual sex is a win-win. He gets his needs met without the risk of falling in love. He's built for casual sex. Remember the Coolidge Effect in the Chapter 5? A man's dopamine goes up, he pursues, reaches his goal, and then his dopamine goes back down. When his dopamine drops, he loses interest in his pursuit. The Coolidge Effect is why men can come on so strong, pursue you so hard, then one day just disappear.

The biggest problem for some women is that he doesn't disappear completely. Now that she's in love, he's free to return as many times as he wants, often chasing other women in between.

---

*Why Some Men Disappear: The Coolidge Effect can cause a man to vanish after he gets sex. Once the challenge is over, his desire and incentive to pursue disappear unless dopamine increases.*

---

## WHY DOESN'T HE JUST SAY HE DOESN'T WANT A RELATIONSHIP?

I often have women ask me, "If he doesn't want a real relationship, why doesn't he just tell me?" There are several reasons for this. First, he has no incentive to tell you. If you don't tell him you're looking for a relationship, he thinks you're simply enjoying your time with him. Second, as long as he's having sex, it's tough for him to stop.

Sexual arousal, especially orgasm, deactivates regions of the prefrontal cortex.[144] This is the area where his morals and ethics are housed. Therefore, a woman might believe that he should know he's stringing her along and feel bad about it. And she would be right, if his brain was fully functional. However, with his morals off-line, he's simply oblivious and having a good time. In fact, chances are good that if she brings up the topic, he probably hasn't even thought of it. The problem is that he can't; that part of his brain is not working that well when she's around him.

As I was explaining this concept during an interview, the interviewer interrupted me.

"Wait a minute. You mean he doesn't know I want to be in an exclusive relationship?" she asked.

"He might have an idea. But unless you make it a requirement, he's probably not going to broach the subject," I said.

"A requirement?" she asked.

"Yes, something that you need for him to be in a relationship with you. Men understand and actually like requirements. It lets them know what they need to do, and it also reassures them that you have standards," I said.

"Why are standards important?"

"When you have standards, specific codes of principles, it sends him the message that you can be trusted when he's not around. This is important, because if he commits to you, in a way, he's giving up some of his power. He needs to know you aren't going to abuse it," I replied.

"Whoa! In that case, I'm going to tell my boyfriend tonight that I want a commitment of exclusiveness," she said.

"Great," I said.

"And if he doesn't give it to me, we're through," she added.

"That might not be a good idea," I said.

"Why not? You said I needed to share my standards," she said.

"Yes, but there's a big difference between having standards and giving an ultimatum. He can't be coerced into this. If he commits under duress, it may not have the same effect on his neurotransmitters. In other words, he's saying 'yes' with his mouth but the rest of him may not be following," I said.

"Well, then, what should I do?" she asked.

"Are you already sleeping with him?" I asked.

"Yes," she said.

"Tell him you really want to be in an exclusive relationship and you completely understand if he doesn't," I said.

"What if nothing happens?" she asked.

"Give it a couple of weeks and if he doesn't respond, you can add a time limit to it. Say something like, 'I would like an answer from you; let me know by the end of the month,'" I suggested.

After a couple of weeks, I checked back with her to see what had happened. She said at first he didn't say anything; he just looked at her like he had heard her words. The next day and the rest of the week he was rather aloof. She thought for sure he was going to break up with her. She started to feel anxious but reminded herself that she desired to be in an exclusive relationship, and if he wasn't interested, then she'd rather break up.

After about a week, he said he would like to be exclusive, if she would. His hesitation was to be expected. This is a big decision for a man to make. In fact, if he doesn't struggle, you should be leery. Men should be afraid to fall in love.

## WHO'S AFRAID OF LOVE?

The idea that men might be afraid of love is completely foreign to most women. Men are bigger and stronger. The average man usually outweighs a woman, even doubling her numbers on the scale. Women view men as protectors and soldiers. Men kill the scary spiders and venomous snakes. They get up in the middle of the night and move in the direction of that menacing noise.

If a woman breaks down on the side of the road, she doesn't call a girlfriend, she calls a man. Her French-tip-manicured girlfriend in Jimmy Choo shoes is no match for those air-wrenched lug nuts. This is a moment when only an unshaven, greasy-handed man with the name "Earl" scribed on his chest will do.

A woman looks at a man and can't conceive what could possibly scare him. Even the thought of someone pulling a gun on our hero can produce images of Clint Eastwood–like defiance, as she imagines him squinting and growling, "Make my day." Therefore, the idea that this behemoth, this pillar of strength and fortitude, would fear something as sweet and innocent as love is mind-boggling. How could Superman be afraid of a little love?

But he is. Love is his kryptonite. Love is the only thing that can take him from his mighty station in his Fortress of Solitude all the way down to his knees. To a woman, love gives safety and security. When a man loves her, she has a worker, a partner, and a protector. Because of that, to a woman, love is empowering.

But to a man, love can be crippling, something he both desperately wants and deeply fears at the same time. Why would a man, a symbol of strength, be afraid of something so wonderful and inoffensive as love?

> *The moment a man gives in to the idea of love—*
> *not sex—but actually gives in to the idea of falling in love*
> *with someone, he begins to lose his power and strength.*

His mighty mojo juice of male potency—testosterone—begins to take a nosedive. When he thinks of those three little words, "I love you," it's as if an air raid siren goes off in his head, followed by the sound of a plane spinning out of control. His manufacturer of muscle mass begins to dry up. He becomes a spinachless Popeye.

It's during this time that a man will hesitate and pull back, even if he's been coming on strong for a long time. Men are naturally reluctant to fall in love. In fact, if he doesn't hesitate, you should be worried. In a study that looked at online love scams, researchers found that "once contact is made, things get intense fast . . . at a very early stage the scammer declares their love for the victim."[145] Does this mean that when he says he loves you, it's a lie? Not at all. But if he wants to vow his undying commitment before the first kiss, you might want to be concerned.

> *Because of his drop in testosterone, a man should have*
> *a natural hesitation to falling in love.*

If he believes he's ready for that drop in testosterone, he'll come back stronger. However, if he still has things to do in his life, such as finish school, find the job he wants, or reach a level in his personal or professional career, he may not come back . . . yet.

The man who's trying to achieve something in his life still needs the strength, stamina, and vitality that his testosterone gives him. He may still want to be with you, but he may not be able to give you the type of commitment that you want at the moment. If it's simply a commitment for exclusivity, some may take the gamble. But if you want marriage and children, he may grapple with "taking the plunge" (as in his testosterone). Of course, this doesn't always mean never; it just means not now.

This time period can be complicated by what's happening with the woman. As she's getting to know a man, her oxytocin level rises. Instead of becoming leery like a man, oxytocin puts duct tape over her amygdala's mouth. She can't see anything wrong. Life is wonderful and ripe for falling in love. If a man starts to pull back, this can cause her to panic.

Her distress is compounded by the fact that a component of his sweat, androstenedione, a component of testosterone, is causing her cortisol levels to rise.[146] When he pulls back, her oxytocin levels can drop, ripping the duct tape off the mouth of her amygdala. Combine this with her higher stress hormone levels, and she can become a nervous wreck. It's as if she's waltzing across the dance floor of life and someone suddenly stops the music. She's left standing there, bewildered and disappointed, like someone left without a seat in musical chairs. She's desperate to get the music playing again, hoping that when it does, all will be well.

It's during this time when a woman may try to tempt or even chase after her man. Sometimes, in her desire to restart the music, she may compromise her own principles. Instead of waiting for that commitment of exclusivity, she may tell herself, "This is close enough." Or, "I want to be with him, so let's have sex and see where it goes." The wait time can simply create too much anxiety for her to bear. But compromising her integrity during this time can be a *huge* mistake.

> *It's natural for a man to hesitate before committing.*

While working on this book, I reconnected with Susanne, an old high school friend, on Facebook. We were chatting via text-messaging when she asked, "What are you working on now?" I wrote back and said, "I'm working on a new book about the science of love. Right now, I'm looking at the biological significance of the advice of dating books, such as *The Rules*." Her response to that was almost eerie. She didn't respond for a minute or two, and when she finally wrote back, all her message said was "Call me," with her number.

I called and asked, "What's wrong?"

"I did *The Rules*," she quickly confessed.

"Really?"

"Yes, I did the *The Rules* on Mark," she whispered.

"You've been married for seven years. Why are you whispering?" I asked.

"I don't know," she laughed.

"So tell me what happened."

"Well, Mark and I were dating causally, but I wanted to get married again. The girls were young and I wanted someone who wanted to be a husband and a father, not just my boyfriend. I told him I wanted more of a commitment."

"So is that when he asked you to marry him?" I asked.

"No," she said. "Nothing happened."

"Since we didn't seem to be moving forward, I decided to make myself less available. I stopped going to his house, stopped making myself available for dates on short notice, stopped calling him, and even stopped returning some of his calls. At first I was nervous, but then one day as I was leaving for work, I found a note on my car from Mark. He lives about thirty minutes away, so he had to put some effort into this. After a while, I was getting notes all the time. He even left them in plastic zipper bags so they wouldn't get wet in the rain or snow. He began asking me out on dates well in advance, and when I wasn't with him, I stayed busy away from home, since I knew he was coming by. After a few months of dating like this, he popped the question. We've been happily married for more than seven years."

What Susanne experienced was Mark's internal struggle. When she pulled away, he felt the loss, but was the loss of the relationship greater than the loss of his testosterone? That's the question he needed to figure out on his own before he could make a commitment. Susanne was smart not to put pressure on Mark. She simply stated what she wanted, and when he didn't step up to give it to her, she slowly began to see him less and less. If he decided not to take the relationship to the next level, Susanne was fully prepared to move on. This is the key. She didn't spout unsupported ultimatums. She knew what she wanted and she knew her worth. She knew she was the prize and had decided that for Mark to "win" her, he needed to propose marriage.

At this point, Mark had to reevaluate the relationship. Remember what a date is: designating a time to evaluate. He had discovered what a relationship with Susanne would be like. Now he needed to figure out if the gain of the relationship was worth the losses of his freedom.

Since the two had already been in a relationship for a while, a new factor entered into his evaluation. Researchers at the University of California found that people are more sensitive to the possibility of losing something than they are to the possibility of gaining something.[147] In other words, the possibility of gaining a marriage was less of a motivator to Mark than the possibility of losing the prize.

Susanne let him decide on his own. She was firm but gentle. You can't make a man fall in love with you by forcing a commitment. He has to freely choose. In fact, if Susanne had been aggressive about it, he might have walked away. An aggressive stance on her part could make Mark feel that a commitment was too risky. When he commits, his dropping testosterone will naturally make him more passive, therefore aggression on her part could make that vulnerability feel too dangerous.

She was falling in love and wanted him to join her. Here's a critical point: Let him debate on his own. Don't pester him, compromise your beliefs, or chase after him. And most of all, don't worry. As a woman falls in love and her oxytocin level rises, it increases trust. He's looking for signs that you trust him.

Susanne had already been in a relationship, so when she decided that she was looking for marriage and not just a boyfriend, she had to pull back, which can be tough. Because of all the hormonal changes that are going on during dating, it's hard to put the brakes on and draw a line about the level of intimacy you're prepared to engage in. Many dating experts tell you to wait to have sex, but one of the biggest debates is how long you should wait. Let's explore this further.

## THE NINETY-DAY RULE

As I discussed in Chapter 5, delaying sex helps a man fall in love. In *Act Like a Lady, Think Like a Man*, author Steve Harvey's signature advice is something he calls "the Ninety-Day Rule," which involves dating and getting to know someone *without* having sex for ninety days.

As we've learned earlier in the book, for a man to fall in love, he must build up a higher level of vasopressin over time, meaning he has to get repeatedly aroused without climaxing. The exact time it takes will vary from man to man. Harvey's rationale for waiting ninety days to give "the cookie" (his cute euphemism for "the nookie") isn't based on extensive scientific research or psychological studies; instead, his justification for waiting ninety days follows the business model of Ford Motor Company. I hope it goes without saying that Ford Motor Company doesn't provide sex; however, it does provide benefits to its employees after a ninety-day probationary period. Harvey says, "Ford's policy was that you had to work at least ninety days before they'd cover your health insurance; this was the plant management saying to me, we will provide you benefits after you have proven to me you are worthy—work hard, show up on time, follow your supervisor's orders, and get along with your co-workers for ninety days, and then you can get dental and medical coverage."

In a similar fashion, Harvey recommends that a woman wait to give up the cookie until a man proves himself worthy to her. In fact, Harvey says, "If you're giving your benefits to a guy who's only been on the job for a week or two, you're making a mistake." It turns out that this is not only wise advice but also biologically sound advice. How long does it take for a man to build up the neurotransmitters to fall in love? A study published in *Cross-Cultural Research* found it takes American men from two months to a year to fall in love.[148] Therefore, the ninety-day rule covers the minimum time period while providing a safety buffer.

> *The longer a man waits to have sex*
> *with a woman he's sexually attracted to, the more*
> *likely he'll fall in love with her.*

A man doesn't fall into the grips of true love overnight. Yes, he may fall in "love" with the physicality of the yummy eye candy standing in front of him, but true love—the "I want to be with you and only you" kind—takes time. If a man is only interested in the dopamine effect, he'll most likely become uncomfortable before the ninety days have passed and wander off in search of a piece of eye candy whose requirements are not so high.

There might be another important reason to wait to have sex if you're looking for love. Researchers at Florida State University found that just because oxytocin or vasopressin is present doesn't mean the receptors are there. Without the receptors, the neurotransmitter can't produce its effect. Your body produces the receptors once the neurotransmitter is present. In a process called epigenesis, your body basically builds receptors based on need. Therefore, as the levels of vasopressin and oxytocin rise, your body sends out

the alert to create new receptors, which are then filled by the neurotransmitter. This, of course, takes some time.[149]

I've mentioned over and over again that a man is resistant to
falling in love. To some women, this idea is just crazy. But it's not.
The real craziness starts when he actually lets go and falls in love.

# PART III

# LOSING YOUR MIND

# CHAPTER

# FALLING IN LOVE

This is it. This is the feeling you have been searching for, that euphoric *I can't sleep, I can't eat, and I can't stop smiling and dancing* splendor. This entire book has been leading up to this point. This is that moment that so many writers and artists have tried to understand, the place Senator William Proxmire said was better left to "poets and mystics, to Irving Berlin, and to thousands of high school and college bull sessions."[150] It's the thing you've been searching for, that unique, indescribably delicious, joyful insanity we crave called *falling in love*.

Somewhere during the dating phase, neurotransmitters increase, causing your body to produce more receptors, which are filled with those neurotransmitters until they reach a pinnacle. On the other side of this, you fall in love and lose your mind. Sounds so romantic, doesn't it? Well, it really is.

Romance is an idealized view of reality, an altered view acquired through love's magical porthole of temporary insanity. When you fall in love, parts of your brain shut down, which allows both partners to get past their fears and become vulnerable. This puts you both in a position of maximum togetherness. Mother Nature lowers your resistance and makes you neurotic, obsessed, excited, and foolish: here is a person who thinks you're the most amazing creature on this planet, and—lucky you—you just happen to feel the same way about them.

## CRAZY LITTLE THING CALLED LOVE

When two people fall in love, it can be like announcing the winner on a game show. As the victor is proclaimed, the lights start flashing, confetti falls from the rafters, and helium balloons are released—as friends and family run up onstage to hug and kiss the winner. The light over the losing opponent is turned off, and he or she is quickly whisked offstage. Then theme music plays as the camera follows the visibly excited winner, as he or she gushes over the prizes.

The mental image you just formed is a lot like what happens in a brain that's high on love. Certain parts of it are dimmed and taken off-line, while other supercharged regions take center stage. Some neurotransmitters drop like falling confetti, while others rise like helium balloons. You bubble and gush with enthusiasm as you realize you have won the ultimate evolutionary grand prize—you have fallen in love.

Inside your skull, your serotonin level plunges while your cortisol level skyrockets. Your oxytocin level reaches an all-time high. If you're a man, your testosterone level plummets. If you're a woman, your testosterone level surges. Your amygdala goes on vacation and takes the Judge, your ventromedial prefrontal cortex, with it. Normal brain activity shifts. This upheaval is facilitated by the release of a type of "Miracle-Gro," which causes new circuits to be formed.

There is a flood of activity, but you're not concerned with any of this because you're pleasantly distracted. As your brain is being rewired, all you want to do is roll around in bed, kissing, nuzzling, and delighting in the knowledge that you have just discovered the most perfect person in the world for you. This is the masterpiece of magnificence you have been looking for all your life. You may even feel like this beautiful creature has somehow provided a piece of you that you felt you were missing. As long as you're with your cuddle bunny, you feel whole, complete, and loved. When your darling is close, life is wonderfully and effortlessly sweet.

It's amazing. But it's also absolutely insane.

## PARTS OF YOUR BRAIN ARE DEACTIVATED

Falling in love delivers a sort of one-two punch to your brain. It causes "large portions of thinking parts of the brain, including the frontal, parietal and middle temporal cortexes, to be deactivated."[151] This is important, so let me repeat it: vast sections of the highly revered, thinking part of your brain are shut down, turned off, go off-line, stop functioning, etcetera—you get my point? That's right: your grand culmination of human evolution first grows dim and then falls asleep. You're officially love-struck (or should I say dumbstruck?).

Not only that, but the parts of your brain needed for critical judgment are also gone. While you were dating, your ventromedial prefrontal cortex (your Judge) and your amygdala were highly active. They were busy evaluating your potential lover and sounding the alarm if necessary. But once you fall in love, all that changes.

Andreas Bartels, at the University of London, found that the judge and the amygdala both become deactivated.[152] They are sent on a much-needed vacation. Once you fall in love, your decision has been made. You have selected the person you want to be with and there's no turning back. Therefore, Mother Nature dismisses your Judge, since you're no longer in need of adjudication. And just to remove any doubt, Mother Nature removes your alarm system too. This is why the dating phase is so critical. Once you fall in love, you will lose all objectivity.

> *It's important to carefully choose while dating,*
> *because when you fall in love, the parts of your brain*
> *that judge and protect are not functioning.*

This can be a nightmare, because you can no longer see any of your beloved's faults. If you don't conduct a careful evaluation during the courtship phase, the mental short-circuiting that happens during this phase can make you miss an important shortcoming. As British neurobiologist Semir Zeki muses, "When deeply in love, we suspend those critical judgments that we otherwise use to assess other people. We are often surprised by the choice of a partner that someone makes, asking futilely whether they have taken leave of their senses. In fact, they have."[153]

This can also be a very beautiful thing, for you no longer see any of your beloved's faults. Pat Mumbay, professor at the Department of Psychiatry and Behavioral Neurosciences and codirector of the Loyola Sexual Wellness Clinic at Loyola University Stritch School of Medicine, explains, "The phrase 'love is blind' is a valid notion because we tend to idealize our partner and see only things that we want to see in early stages of the relationship. Outsiders may have a much more objective and rational perspective on the partnership than the two people involved do."[154]

Andreas Bartels, at the University of London, found that the area of your brain* involved in "theory of mind" tasks, that is, the ability to distinguish one's desires, beliefs, and intentions from another person's, also become deactivated.[155] You can no longer distinguish your dreams and desires from your beloved's. It's as if you both want the same exact things from life. Your goals are his goals.

Fortunately, the London researchers describe this phenomena as a selective suspension. You can still judge the quality of a book or another person. You also have the ability to have theory of mind with another person, as long as that person is not your beloved. It appears that the deactivation only happens with the one you love.[156]

This deactivation of your inner judge is important. Your judge is what separates you from other people. When your judge is active, you may say to yourself, "I'm better than them; they are better than me; I'm prettier, uglier, smarter, dumber, more than, less than," and so on. You judge yourself as different in some way from other people. But when your judge is mute, it can feel as if there is no difference, you're alike, the same; it's as if you're one with your beloved.

This anomaly can be an affirming characteristic, similar to that of a mother gazing at her perfect child. You can't see your beloved's faults. He or she is flawless in your eyes. When you're looking at each other, you see nothing but a magnificent being. You both feel this reflected in each other. It's this quality of falling in love that provides warmth and love, as well as nurturing esteem, to the recipient. It can be a magical gift exchanged by a couple.

---

*This area includes the medial prefrontal cortex, the parietal temporal junction, and the temporal poles.

Interestingly, one study found that the level of deactivation may predict longevity. In a joint study conducted by several New York universities and universities in China, researchers found that couples who stayed together for forty months after the beginning of a relationship showed less activation of the ventromedial prefrontal cortex (your Judge) early in the relationship.[157] In other words, when your Judge is still very active early in the relationship, the chances of you staying together are lessened. Thus, at this point in the relationship, between six months and one year, if you're still having doubts, chances are pretty good the relationship may not last.

> *Lingering doubts within a relationship*
> *between the span of six months to one year are*
> *indications of relationship trouble.*

There's one more thing that happens when your Judge deactivates. It's not just the ability to judge your beloved's actions that you lose, but you also lose the ability to judge your own. Sometimes the craziest things seem reasonable and prudent. You may rationalize skipping work so you two can spend the day in bed together, giggling that you really are sick (lovesick, that is). Love can make you do strange things—things that would not be within the realm of consideration during any other time in your life.

Take, for example, the case of Joseph Andrew Dekenipp. On February 14, 2014, Joseph scaled two twelve-foot-high fences, crawled through skin-shredding razor wire, and added multiple years to his less-than-one-year sentence to break out of jail in Pinal County, Arizona.

Now, this may not seem surprising. You might think *a lot of people try to break out of jail*. But Joseph didn't break out of jail with a well-thought-out escape plan or with the intention of hiding from the law and starting a new life. No, Joseph took a relatively minor sentence and drastically compounded it by breaking out to have a very brief Valentine's Day dinner with his sweetheart in public. That's right; this love-drunk Prince Charming didn't try to hide his love. In fact, he was arrested just three hours after his daring escape. He was found having a romantic dinner with his girlfriend at the Gallopin' Goose Saloon and Grill, just thirteen miles away from the jail.

He was easy to find because "Officials said he told inmates he was broken-hearted being away from his girlfriend for so long."[158] They just had to find her to find him. Love can make you lose your mind; you can "rationalize" spending several more long years locked up just to have a few precious minutes with your lover on Valentine's Day.

Your ventromedial prefrontal cortex is also involved with something scientists call self-processing. That's the ability to understand "mine" from "not mine" or "me" from "not me."[159] When your Judge is off-line, you feel less like separate people and more connected. There is no longer "mine" and "his" but "ours." This is where you move from "him and me" to "us." It's as if you and your beloved become one.

In addition, when you fall in love, activity in your frontal lobe is temporarily suspended.[160] This means more than just your Judge, the larger thinking part of your brain, is debilitated; you can even lose the ability to concentrate. As researcher Henk van Steenbergen from Leiden University discovered, the more in love you are, the less focused you become. In his study, forty-three participants who had been in love for six months or less were asked to perform a number of tasks where they had to discriminate irrelevant information from relevant information. He found that the more intensely in love a person was, the less he or she was able to focus on the task. The intensity and lack of focus appeared to be most acute in the beginning of the relationship. In response to his findings, Van Steenbergen stated, "When you have just become involved in a romantic relationship you'll probably find it harder to focus on other things, because you spend a large part of your cognitive resources on thinking of your beloved."[161]

But let's get back to the good parts again for just a moment. Because some of these deactivated areas—the cortical zone, along with the parietal cortex and parts of the temporal lobe—are commonly involved in negative emotions, you see the world differently.[162] Those old negative voices that told you you're not good enough are quieted. This is one of the greatest things about being in love. You feel amazing, relieved of the burden of negativity. In fact, Bartels observed that deactivation of these areas have proven to be a successful treatment against depression.[163]

It's as if you've become a star in your own animated movie. Pharrell Williams glides out singing *Happy*, as you walk, with birds flying around your head and small woodland creatures bounding over to greet you.

## HIS TESTOSTERONE

Recall that a man can be reluctant about falling in love because once he does, his testosterone level takes a nosedive. The biological fact that testosterone levels fall is enough to indicate that love is much more than just sex.

Testosterone increases following sexual intercourse.[164] Since young lovers tend to be quite amorous, you would expect to see a rise (yes, both physically and hormonally). As Anil Ananthaswamy states in *New Scientist*, "If love was just about sex, we would expect the man's testosterone to increase and stay high." [165] However, it doesn't. It does just the opposite. During this phase of love, a man's testosterone levels plummet.

The ancient story of Samson and Delilah teaches us a valuable biological lesson. In the story, Samson had superhuman strength, like a man with turbocharged testosterone. But he also had two weaknesses: an attraction to an untrustworthy woman and his hair. If Samson cut his hair, he would lose his physical strength.

When Samson fell in love with Delilah, he made the mistake of telling her the secret of his strength. After learning of his weakness, Delilah betrayed Samson and made a deal with his enemies. In exchange for riches, she cut off Samson's hair, causing him to become as weak as any other man. Now that Samson had lost his superhuman strength, he could be seized.

The subtle biological moral to the story is that when a man falls in love, he becomes vulnerable—his strength diminishes. His source of strength, his testosterone, decreases. The real story of Samson and Delilah was that Delilah really never had to do anything, because as soon as Samson fell in love, he was already a goner.

Although testosterone tends to drop with a committed relationship, there is something else that can cause his hormone to free-fall even further. There is something else that can zap his strength, something that can devastate his masculinity. What is it? Fatherhood.

As Professor Gangestad at the University of New Mexico states, "Probably the most effective way, short of castration, for men to reduce testosterone levels is to have a child." [166] This, of course, makes biological sense. A mother and child's survival increases if she has the father to help her. Therefore, Mother Nature helps her out by lowering his testosterone even further. This lowering of his testosterone appears to have a protective effect for the relationship. With lower testosterone, a man is less sexually attracted and less likely to want to compete for a new woman's attention. In addition, even if he wanted to fool around, he might have some trouble. Not only has his stamina been zapped, his lower testosterone is probably shrinking his hippocampus. If you recall, the hippocampus is where he stores his directional memory of where all the women are located. Therefore, as a man commits to one woman, the other women's locations slowly fade away.

This loss of testosterone is not as bad as it first looks. In a Harvard University study, Peter Gray and his team decided to sample the testosterone of both single and committed men at different points throughout the day. Their results confirmed that committed men (not necessarily married) have lower testosterone levels than single men. However, interestingly, the team found that committed men had lower testosterone levels only in samples collected later in the day. It appeared that all the men woke up with relatively high testosterone levels, but by the day's end, the committed men's levels dropped substantially, while the single guys' levels remained the same.[167]

This makes perfect biological sense. Our committed guy still needs to get out and hunt, protect, and generally get some work done. But right around sunset, when the single guy's ready to go out and party, our committed guy is losing his stamina and probably some memory. Instead of going out and competing with the other men, the lower testosterone in the committed guy makes him feel more like going home. By cutting his testosterone, Mother Nature fuels his incentive to return to his family. Why would he go out with rapidly dwindling testosterone and try to compete against fully fortified men for a new woman when he has a perfectly good woman waiting at home?

In addition, if you recall, he has a special spot in this hypothalamus called the "pursuit spot." This is what activates his chase behavior. His pursuit spot is sensitive to testosterone. Therefore, as his levels drop, his pursuit spot starts to shrink.[168] This further zaps his desire to chase others.

Now, you might be wondering, "Would his lower testosterone affect his sex life?" That would be a great concern, since you know that testosterone and sexual desire are linked. But Mother Nature has an answer for that also. A study from the University of Glasgow in the United Kingdom found that the combination of dopamine and oxytocin has a positive influence on male sexual activity, including penile erection.[169] In other words, as these two other neurotransmitters increase when he falls in love, it appears they may help compensate for the lower testosterone. Now that our committed and in-love guy has lower testosterone, it allows oxytocin to have an effect.

## STUCK ON YOU WITH OXYTOCIN

In a joint study with Yale University and Gonda Multidisciplinary Brain Research Center at Bar-Ilan University in Israel, researchers looked at the effect that falling in love had on oxytocin. The researchers examined the plasma oxytocin levels of 120 new lovers (60 couples) three months after the initiation of their romantic relationships and compared the levels to 43 unattached singles. The study found that the couples had higher oxytocin levels than singles.

Then, the couples who stayed together were retested to see what effect (if any) it had on oxytocin. They found that the oxytocin levels of the couples who stayed together remained elevated during the first six months of the relationship.[170] Those results were not very surprising; however, Ruth Feldman, one of the researchers in the study, did find something extraordinary. Not only were the oxytocin levels highest in new lovers, she noted that "the increase in oxytocin during the period of falling in love was the highest that we've ever found."[171] It was so high, in fact, that new lovers had almost double the normal levels of oxytocin, even compared to pregnant women, whom you would expect to have the highest.

Even more significant than the dramatically high levels was the effect it had on couples. When couples were asked to share positive experiences, Feldman found that high-oxytocin couples were more attuned to each other than low-oxytocin couples. The high-oxytocin couples laughed together, frequently touched each other, and even finished each other's sentences. Feldman believes that these behaviors are linked with oxytocin in a type of positive feedback loop. Positive feedback loops are self-amplifying. As Feldman explains, "Oxytocin can elicit loving behaviors, but giving and receiving these behaviors also promotes the release of oxytocin and leads to more of these behaviors."[172] That's why the levels can rise so astronomically. When a couple smooches, caresses, and coos, they ooze oxytocin, which causes them to kiss, cuddle, and schmooze even more. This then leads to both partners becoming more loving and understanding and to feeling more loved and understood.

The most important finding of the study has to be the information regarding longevity and oxytocin levels. They discovered that couples with the highest levels were the ones who stayed together the longest.[173] In other words, the more oxytocin the couple had, the stronger their love-bonding abilities became.

If you recall, testosterone blocks the effects of oxytocin for men.

Now, that all changes. When a man falls in love, his testosterone decreases, making him more vulnerable to the effects of oxytocin. That once-invincible man of steel is now morphing into a big, soft teddy bear who wants to snuggle with only you. That's right, ladies. Lucky for you, Mother Nature has turned him into a cuddle bunny— make that a monogamous cuddle bunny.

## OXYTOCIN IS PROTECTIVE

Oxytocin appears to also have a protective effect that prevents infidelity. Dr. René Hurlemann, from the University of Bonn in Germany, conducted a study to test oxytocin's effects on a man's faithfulness. She stated, "Because oxytocin is known to increase trust in people, we expected men under the influence of the hormone to allow the female experimenter to come even closer." To test this theory, Hurlemann asked fifty-seven men, some in relationships and some single, to receive a dose of oxytocin nasal spray. What Hurlemann found surprised her. "The direct opposite happened," she said. When men in committed, monogamous relationships were given a dose of oxytocin nasal spray, they kept a larger physical distance—about four to six inches—from attractive women they didn't know compared to men who received a placebo. The oxytocin didn't have any effect on the distance the single men kept between themselves and the attractive women. From her results, Hurlemann has come to believe that oxytocin helps to keep men faithful. She credits high levels of oxytocin, like those experienced when a man falls in love, with helping him to stay loyal, by prompting him to steer clear of attractive women.[174]

What's even more amazing is what Dirk Scheele of Bonn University

Medical Center found. He discovered that, in a sense, oxytocin spellbinds the man into thinking that his woman is the most beautiful in all the land. To test this, Scheele gave a dose of oxytocin to men and conducted brain scans while they viewed pictures of either their partners or other women. He then compared the brain scans to a questionnaire about the perceived attractiveness of each photo's subject. Scheele states, "When the men received oxytocin instead of the placebo, their reward system in the brain when viewing the partner was very active, and they perceived them as more attractive than the other women."[175] That's right, ladies; no need to worry about your hair or makeup. When your lover has a heaping gob of oxytocin, you're guaranteed to be the fairest of them all.

Oxytocin also has an effect on women. When a woman falls in love, the increase in oxytocin makes her more loving, trusting, and less anxious. It helps her to deal with stress better, improves her memory, and gives her a generally positive mood.[176]

## HER TESTOSTERONE

In a strange twist, as *his* testosterone is tumbling downhill, *hers* is sprinting up.[177] While a man is becoming more passive, a woman is becoming more aggressive—sexually aggressive, that is. In women, testosterone increases cause her to become more sexually active. So, as the other boys are talking about heading out for the evening, the newly committed man knows he needs to get home because he left something turned on.

During this time of fresh commitment, most couples can't seem to keep their hands off each other. In other words, they don't call it "making love" for nothing. But although sexual activity is at an all-time high, there is something more subtle going on here. As his testosterone level is going down and hers is going up, in a way, the man is becoming more like the woman and the woman is becoming more like the man. As Donatella Marazziti of the University of Pisa in Italy suggests, falling in love temporarily eliminates some of the differences between the sexes, and softens some male features.[178]

When this happens to you, it can make you feel like the lines that separate you and your romantic partner are blurred. You begin to feel more similar, maybe even like one unit. You can feel a connection and kinship that you have never experienced with anyone else. It can feel like you both know and understand each other so well. Those little differences are temporarily suppressed. You can feel so similar that you know what they'll say before they say it.

It's as if you fall under the grand and wondrous illusion that you and your beloved are one, that you completely understand each other, and that you and this amazing person share the same hopes and dreams. You're convinced that this is the one person who truly appreciates you and wants you to be happy. This may be what Aristotle meant when he said, "Love is composed of a single soul inhabiting two bodies."

## SEROTONIN

We've learned about the importance of ramping up dopamine levels in the dating phase, but it turns out that high, sustained levels of dopamine cause another important shift when you fall in love. Noted British neurobiologist Semir Zeki has linked the increase in dopamine experienced in the dating phase to a subsequent decrease in serotonin when you fall in love.[179] Serotonin, sometimes called the hormone of happiness, plummets during this phase.

Now this might sound alarming. Your hormone of bliss is slipping away. But don't worry; you've got plenty of bliss from other sources (which we'll talk about in a minute). Right now, the drop in serotonin is not about happiness but has a different effect.

When you fall in love, your serotonin level can actually drop to the same level as that of someone suffering from obsessive-compulsive disorder (OCD), a condition characterized by two main features: obsessive or interfering thoughts and compulsive or impulsive urges. A person with OCD can't stop thinking about a particular object or problem, and he or she feels as if something must be done to relieve their looping thoughts.

The difference between more normal behavior and OCD is that with OCD, an individual will end up performing a ritual or behavior over and over again, to the point that it interferes with his or her normal life. It's this trait that OCD shares with new relationships. Early on, couples report having interrupting thoughts about each other. A man might say, "She's all I ever think about," while a woman may announce, "I just can't stop thinking about him."

As forensic psychologist J. Reid Meloy, a professor at the University of California, San Diego, explains, "Lovers think obsessively about the beloved; they cannot get these intrusive thoughts out of their minds." This behavior can be so intense that it can sometimes resemble a pathological condition. In fact, Meloy believes that this is a "trait they most likely share with stalkers."[180]

When you fall in love, those intrusive images and internal commentaries can disrupt your ability to concentrate, to the point of interfering with your daily functions. They're supposed to. As Zeki explains, "Love, after all, is a kind of obsession and in its early stages commonly immobilizes thought and channels it in the direction of a single individual."[181]

When members of a falling-in-love couple are apart, intrusive thoughts swoop in, raising anxiety levels. To relieve the distress this causes, one person is virtually forced to search out the other. This may be the main reason why Mother Nature lowers your serotonin level, so that you two will spend as much time together as possible. And if you happen to be apart, your reduced serotonin level will make this separation so uncomfortable that you'll do just about anything to get back together. But there may be one more reason why your serotonin level crashes: sex.

High levels of serotonin are associated with feelings of happiness and being satiated, which causes a loss of sexual interest because it reduces your sexual appetite.[182] It's not that you don't want sex when serotonin levels are high; it's just that you're not interested *right now*. It's rather like passing a buffet shortly after you've eaten. It's not that the food isn't appetizing or doesn't smell good; it's just that you're not hungry at the moment.

But when your serotonin levels drop, you can feel famished. Now when you walk by the buffet, you start salivating, like Pavlov's dog. You want to run in and eat as much as you can. You just want to gorge on food or, in the case of falling in love, you want to gorge on sex.

Now, if you're thinking, *See, it really is all about sex,* allow me to introduce you to the next neurotransmitter—cortisol.

## CORTISOL

Timothy Loving at the University of Texas in Austin found that the adrenal glands release cortisol (stress hormone) while falling in love. He believes this effect is more pronounced in women. Loving theorizes that the more a woman thinks about or focuses on her relationship, the higher her cortisol levels.

To test his theory, Loving conducted a study on twenty-nine women who had recently fallen "madly, deeply in love," with a relationship duration of less than a year. Salivary cortisol levels were measured as each individual participated in a guided imagery exercise in which she was instructed to either focus on the face of her partner or the face of a friend. The results showed that cortisol levels rose higher when women focused on the faces of their partners rather than on friends' faces. However, when Loving looked at all the variables, he found some significant differences. He discovered that women in the shortest relationships had the highest baseline cortisol levels, relative to women in longer relationships. In other words, when a woman falls in love, her cortisol levels skyrocket but then begin to slowly decrease as the relationship continues.[183]

Loving focused on women in his study "because of the relatively profound role one-on-one relationships play in women's lives relative to men."[184] He believes that women are more vulnerable to cortisol but stops short at suggesting why, biologically, this might be true.

Contrary to Loving's belief, another study found that men are just as vulnerable. And, not only that, women may not be as vulnerable as first believed. Fluctuating hormones of premenopausal women and birth control chemicals can have major influences. In a German study, researcher Clemens Kirschbaum found that men and women show significant differences in cortisol stress responses. He found that gender, the menstrual cycle phase, and the use of oral contraceptives exert important effects on stress in healthy individuals. Salivary cortisol levels were highest in response to stress in women in the luteal phase of her menstrual cycle. That's the phase right after ovulation, up to and including the premenstrual phase. The second highest salivary cortisol levels were found in men, followed by women in the follicular phase of menstruation and preovulation. Women taking oral contraceptives were the least responsive.[185] This finding supports the biological theory that "falling in love" causes a couple to come together at the perfect time to produce a child. The stress response was highest in the fertile women, followed by the men. It was lower in the women who were less likely to conceive and lowest in the women taking medication to prevent pregnancy.

But before you scream "Ah ha, it *is* all about reproduction!" allow me to remind you that although sexual attraction is enhanced by fear-inducing norepinephrine, it's dowsed by cortisol. The stress hormone cortisol can squelch a budding sexual attraction faster than a teenage girl's daddy with a shotgun.

Therefore, the questions that arise are: Why does the cortisol level surge? Why are two people walking around with earth-shattering stress levels when they should be plucking flowers and staring into each other's eyes? Why would Mother Nature make you edgy and anxious instead of serene? This would seem to be characteristic of war, not love.

The reason Mother Nature can amp up levels of our stress hormones is because she has disconnected our stress system. Remember the vacationing amygdala? In this phase of love, you have a strange combination of high anxiety with a quiet amygdala, therefore the stress doesn't cause you to run away but propels you toward your beloved.

The stress causes you to lose your appetite and sleep. You should be running away from the situation, looking for relief, but the part of your brain that tells you to *go* is still on that beach sipping piña coladas. This causes the four Fs of your fight-or-flight response to be limited. Remember the four Fs? *Fight, flight, feed,* or . . . be *friendly.* Yeah, that's it. In this situation you're not running away, you don't want to fight, you can't eat . . . so you're left with one F: fun.

All you want to do is be with the other person, mostly in new and wondrous positions. One day apart (or out of bed) can feel like an eternity. You can experience such separation anxiety that risking your life and years of freedom by breaking out of jail for just a few minutes with your beloved can seem like a reasonable decision.

The only way you can feel some relief from all this crazy anxiety is through sex. Okay, so it may be a little bit about sex. As the old adage goes, "Love creates the tension; sex relieves it." And the next neurotransmitter answers the question of how.

## ENDORPHINS

While a newly fallen-in-love couple is whiling away the hours, delighting in passionate lovemaking, their bodies are producing a type of love drug. During those deliciously inspiring moments of orgasm, your body releases endorphins. Endorphins are nature's "pain relievers." They are opioid-like substances that reduce any physical pain while producing that dreamy enraptured sensation of love.

When you fall in love, your body's release of endorphins makes you feel elated. As Dr. Sean Mackey, chief of the Division of Pain Management at Stanford University School of Medicine says, "When people are in the passionate, all-consuming phase of love, there are significant alterations in their mood that are impacting their experience of pain. Love-induced analgesia may block pain—similar to how opioid analgesics work."[186] With the removal of any pain or fatigue, you feel young, fresh, happy, and strong.

In a somewhat cruel study, scientists inflicted pain on participants to study the effect that love had on an individual's pain level. All participants were still in the first nine months of their relationships (probably to ensure they were still in the insanity phase, because who else would agree to this?). The individuals were asked to look at pictures of either their romantic partners or acquaintances, while their hands were immersed in water at various temperatures, starting at room temperature and moving on to a bowl of painfully hot, near-boiling water. The results showed that viewing a romantic partner compared to an acquaintance significantly reduced the pain that was felt.[187] Ah, this is the soothing balm of love.

As you have sex, you release more endorphins, which cause you to feel great. At the same time, you're releasing sex hormones that cause you to want more sex,[188] which causes you to release more endorphins and more sex hormones, which causes you to feel good and want more sex, and around and around you go. This cycle becomes self-amplifying. You start out having sex in the bed, then in the shower, then you go out to the kitchen to eat breakfast and the next thing you know, you're having sex on the kitchen table. Next, you're having sex on the kitchen floor. You go for a drive and can't wait to get home. Next thing you know, you pull over and have sex in the car. No surface or area is beyond consideration. Just ask Michael Suh and Nicole Germack, a Philadelphia couple that was arrested after being caught having sex on the roof of their neighborhood Chipotle restaurant.[189] I guess they couldn't stop long enough for lunch.

As you're having sex, your system is being flooded with super feel-good, morphine-like chemicals. However, in love, when your cortisol is high, endorphins act differently. They are released in the limbic system, which reduces not just physical pain but also emotional anxiety. Now, not only does the opiate cause any pain to decrease, it also causes the feeling of intense euphoria.[190] It can make you feel like a seven-year-old who's walking into Disney World for the first time. Everything feels exciting and magical.

Your body is at ease, as if you just had a weeklong spa vacation where you were pampered and oiled, your feet massaged, and your body soaked in a warm Jacuzzi bath filled with lavender and jasmine petals. There is a feeling of peace and a serene sense of well-being. You have found your Nirvana, as your brain is washed with a quietly joyful awareness that all is right and perfect in the world.

You now know with the utmost certainty that as long as this enchanted creature is in your life, it will always be wonderful and sweet. This hypnotic intoxication is what people are referring to when they talk about wanting love—a glorious, grounded, and expansive tranquillity. But although you feel captivated, everything is not rosy and tranquil in your brain, as we will see.

## MENTAL MIRACLE-GRO

Falling in love also releases a chemical that has been described as a type of fertilizer or Miracle-Gro for your brain. Part of that sprawling euphoria you experience when you fall in love is due to the expansion of your brain. You release at least two known neurological growth chemicals: nerve growth factor (NGF) and brain-derived neurotropic factor (BDNF). These substances increase and enhance your brain's capacities.

You feel inspired with new ideas and bursts of creative energy. The secretion of these growth factors may be one of the reasons some artists look for a muse. Painters like Picasso would often look for inspiration by finding a young woman to "fall in love" with. This act would cause of surge of growth factors that could revitalize his creativity.

Enzo Emanuele at the University of Pavia in Italy evaluated NGF levels of fifty-eight individuals who had recently fallen in love. The levels were compared to others who were in long-term relationships or who were single. He found that individuals who had recently fallen in love, and who were in relationships with durations of less than six months, had significantly higher NGFs than single people and long-term lovers.[191] Also, it appears that the concentration of NGF correlates with the intensity of romantic feelings. He found it was highest in those couples who said they were "truly, deeply and madly in love."[192] That is to say, the stronger the feeling of love, the greater the nerve growth gush.

Nerve growth factor causes the length of neurons to grow. It's also critical to the survival of existing neurons. Without it, neurons would experience preprogrammed death. In other words, falling in love seems to increase connectivity in your brain and keeps your brain young by allowing more neurons to stay alive. But even with all that, it's not the only brain growth happening here. You still have BDNF, which has a little different effect

Researchers in Cambridge found that BDNF helps women get closer to their beloved by reducing social anxiety and fear of strangers. BDNF, which is induced by estrogen, significantly reduces avoidance behaviors in women.[193] In addition, BDNF plays a role in promoting feelings of well-being when the partner is around.[194]

Researchers at Cambridge University have also explored how BDNF is produced when you fall in love. They discovered that it plays a role in synaptic plasticity. That is to say, it helps your neurons talk to one another. It fosters new connections, which is important for learning and memory. It also helps encourage the growth and differentiation of new neurons and synapses. In other words, it takes your brain from a one-to-one message type of system and converts it to a sort of chat room. It creates more connections, which allows different parts of your brain to communicate with one another. This permits you to tap into new and underutilized regions of your neocortex. You can have new thoughts and inventive ideas.

However, this growth may not be as sweet and innocently delightful as it first appears. There is something almost sinister going on here. In a way, Mother Nature is acting like a drug pusher, helping you to get addicted to love. BDNF, that great brain-enhancing chemical, has also been found to induce drug dependency. Research out of the University of Toronto shows that BDNF appears to make rodents more dependent on opioids.[195] Yes, that's opiates, like those endorphins Mother Nature has been so freely plying you with. In other words, Mother Nature, the master of molecular mixology, appears to be combining endorphins and BDNF in your brain to create an addictive love potion to get a couple hooked on endorphins and, by extension, hooked on each other.

While writing this chapter, I received an e-mail from a former client. Periodically, I receive exciting updates, and this was no exception. Kim wrote to tell me she was starting a thrilling new career in illustration. It was something she had always wanted to do but in the past was not brave enough to pursue. Since starting her relationship with Bo last year, she found the courage to take the risk. Kim's experience is not unusual.

Your Judge not only judges other people, it judges you. While it was on vacation, all of its negative opinions about you were also sequestered. Psychologists Arthur Aron, Elaine Aron (both at the State University of New York at Stony Brook), and Meg Paris (California Graduate School of Family Psychology) discovered that the dramatic, transformative experience of falling in love reshapes your self-concept. Love expands your self-efficacy, or your belief in your own ability to be effective and reach your goals. They also believe that love increases your self-esteem and your overall judgment of your self-worth.[196]

The opinion of that third-grade teacher who said you weren't that bright is gone. The voice of your art teacher who said you lacked imagination has been squashed. Those nagging self-doubts vanish. The harsh voice that says you're "not good enough" is gagged. Like the Bionic Woman, you feel better than you were before—smarter, stronger, and faster. Along with deactivated brain regions, those added endorphins give you a sense of power and control.[197] You have been rebuilt.

All of this leads to self-expansion. Now, no longer being held back by self-doubts, you're open to change and trying new things. Love is not the only risk you're willing to take. Now that you're in a loving relationship, you feel safe to explore new avenues, try new hobbies, and explore new careers. The effect can be particularly profound for individuals suffering from low self-esteem. They will be able to tap into new resources because those nerve factors are causing love to grow and expand their brains.

## HERE'S WHAT'S GOING ON

By now you probably agree with my assertion that falling in love is a type of splendid insanity—a welcomed madness, but a madness nevertheless. But why does this happen? Is there a reason for all of this neurological chaos? What's really going on here? Why are women becoming more like men and men more like women? Why are we stuck on each other while displaying neurotic, obsessive-compulsive anxiety when separated? Why would Mother Nature hijack our brains with intrusive thoughts and turn off the thinking abilities and structures that are critical to our safety and survival? Really, what the hell is Mother Nature thinking?

## INSANITY HELPS YOU GET CLOSE

All these factors—the loss of critical judgment, the silencing of your alarm system, high cortisol keeping you close, oxytocin causing you to want to cuddle, OCD-like obsession from the loss of serotonin and the addictive endorphins—come together in a perfectly orchestrated aim: to decrease your resistance to love.

As neurobiologist Zeki notes, "There is a reason for the madness . . . which serves a higher purpose of uniting unlikely pairs."[198] Think about it: Mother Nature wants us to mix up our chromosomes. In order to promote this, she causes you to be attracted to your opposite. This means that your biologically perfect mate is very different from you, a person with completely different chromosomes, lacking any of your recessive traits. Maybe even someone from the other side of the world.

Barring any family and societal pressure pushing you toward a specific type of individual, you would most likely pick someone who looks and sounds very different from yourself. Psychiatrist Donatella Marazziti explains it well: "The real paradox [is that] humans are attracted to, courted by and breed with genetically unrelated individuals whom they would otherwise instinctively avoid."[199]

This becomes evident when you take a closer look at the effects of the neurotransmitters that are released. Cortisol, oxytocin, and NGF are all known to help overcome neophobia, or the fear of new situations and new people,[200] while BDNF is believed to play a role in decreasing avoidance and fear of unfamiliar people in women. In other words, it lowers a woman's apprehension and allows her to get closer to her partner. All these chemicals doing similar things may seem a bit like overkill, but Mother Nature wants you to love and be loved. And to be certain that her wishes are carried out, she orchestrates a tsunami of neurochemical bravado that should successfully snuff out any niggling uncertainty you're feeling about your partner.

For a brief moment, it can almost feel as if you're infinite. That feeling of boundless harmony happens when your defenses and resistance are temporarily suspended. This amazing synergy not only makes you feel as if you're one with your partner, you adopt a sense that you're directly connected to the world—to the plants, the animals, and maybe even to God.

But there has to be more than just genetic diversity at play here. Other animals don't fall in love yet still manage diversity. If it's simply about genetic diversity, that could be accomplished with an instinct. Therefore, there must be more going on.

PART IV

# FINDING LOVE

# CHAPTER

# REAL LOVE

There you are, wrapped in the warm blanket of love bliss. You've found the perfect person for you, and you've made a commitment to each other. Maybe you've even made a commitment that included "until death do we part." The past several months together have been amazing, to the point of annoying a few friends with your cooing and cuddling.

But then one day, you wake up to notice that something has changed. You start noticing things about your beloved that you had missed before. Maybe it's the first time you heard him snore, or the first time you disagreed on what to eat, or maybe you saw him smacking his lips when he ate his cereal. You find this new behavior quite irritating.

Slowly, your magical haze of ecstasy begins to fade. You might even notice the Pharrell Williams *Happy* song has stopped playing. As the days go on, you realize it's not as simple as a few new, unpleasant behaviors. It appears that your love bunny may have changed. That little thing he used to do that was so endearing just embarrassed you in front of your friends. In fact, some things that you previously thought were charming have now become alarming.

You start to have doubts and ask yourself, *What's happening? Is our love over? Is he not the one? Have I made a mistake?* No, you've just begun the transition into the next phase of love. Didn't realize there was another phase after falling in love? What? You bought that line that says all you had to do was locate "the one" and you'll live happily ever after? Yeah, a lot of us do. We thought you fell in love and stayed in that ecstasy forever. Damn Hollywood and romance novels!

## HOW LONG?

A friend of mine recently got married. A couple of weeks after the ceremony, I ran into her. She knew about the work I was doing and asked if she could ask a question. I said, "Sure." Then her body language changed. She looked around like she didn't want anyone to hear and then whispered, "How long?"

"How long what?" I whispered back.

"How long do we have?"

She had heard me talk many times about how falling in love is temporary insanity. She was still basking in the glow of her recent nuptials and didn't want it to end.

"You have about two years," I said. She looked disappointed.

I then said, "Don't worry. This is just the end of one phase. There's a better stage waiting if you choose it."

## WHAT'S HAPPENING?

In a study on the hormonal changes that happen when people fall in love, Donatella Marazziti, professor of psychiatry and director of the psychopharmacology laboratory at the Department of Psychiatry, Neurobiology, Pharmacology, and Biotechnology at the University of Pisa, measured the initial hormone levels of people who had fallen in love and then later measured those levels again. She wanted to see if the hormone levels had changed after a certain period of time and, if they had, what the time frame was.

She went back to her original couples and measured the cortisol levels of couples who had stayed together. All of the couples had been together between twelve to eighteen months and reported that they were no longer feeling the crazy initial mental state. The couples were now feeling calmer and no longer obsessed.

Marazziti's new measurements showed that the couple's hormones had returned to normal. These new hormone levels were no different than those levels observed in the control group. In fact, Marazziti discovered that in all those tested, all hormonal differences dissipated when the subjects were retested between twelve to twenty-four months later.[201] Because of this, she concluded that "falling in love seems to have a precise time course, with an average duration of between 18 months and 3 years."[202]

In addition to the hormone analysis, researchers at Stony Brook University performed fMRI brain scans on individuals who were in a long-term relationship and compared those scans with early love. They chose couples who had been together for at least ten years. They found that some of the neural activation was the same for both early and long-term love. However, there were some important differences between the brain scans of early-love couples compared to couples in long-term love. These differences were observed in the previously deactivated areas of their brains.

As we discovered earlier, when you fall in love, brain scans show deactivation of parts of your cortex, including the ventromedial prefrontal cortex (your Judge) and the amygdala. Now all this changes. Where early love showed deactivation of the amygdala and the Judge, long-term love not only showed reactivation, it showed significant activation.[203] This means that when these two structures come back online, they may start trying to make up for lost time. You go from being peaceful and quietly nonjudgmental to being superanalytical and critical.

In addition, remember those huge chunks of your neocortex that were deactivated when you fell in love? Well, they're back. Recall that one of the sleeping parts of your brain was in the "theory of mind" area that separated your dreams and goals from your beloved. This area is now alive and active. This means that all those dreams you were sure you two shared as you were sitting up all night talking about the future begin to show some separation. You start to notice little fractures in cohesiveness.

He might not be as wild about painting the house lavender as you are. Or you might not be as keen to cash out the 401(k) to invest in vintage muscle cars as he expected. Slowly, you both might realize that you really are two separate people. The soul-mate image of two people sharing one heart begins to wither. In some couples this new reality can be too much. In fact, Helen Fisher found in her research that the majority of divorces in the United States happen around two years of marriage.[204]

## THE RETURN

When your Judge starts making negative verdicts about you or your beloved, it can trigger your amygdala. This increasing anxiety can cause you to start having doubts. You might begin asking yourself, *Was I wrong about him?* You may start getting nervous. You might even call a friend and voice your concerns out loud. Slowly, your conviction and trust, which were so strong not that long ago, begin to erode.

Maybe you find yourself snooping around his computer or Facebook page. You find yourself straining to see his screen when his phone rings. It can get so bad that you might start think about tracking him with GPS. Or maybe things have changed in a different way. You start noticing that he's not trying as hard as he used to. Maybe you've married or moved in together and his personal habits are not to your liking.

After the publication of my first book, I had a group of women who met at my house. Every week they would bound in, ready for a new evening—all except for one. Nikki, a thin woman with long, dark hair, would trudge to her usual location on the couch and sit in bristling silence.

Every week I would ask her how she was doing and every week she gave the same reply: "How could he do this?" she would say through pursed lips. "He was such an asshole. I tried to tell him, but he wouldn't listen."

Nikki met her soon-to-be ex-husband, Dick, through a mutual friend. I'm not sure if that was his real name or her pet name for him. Anyway, Dick was divorced with two children. They had a whirlwind romance, marrying within the first year of dating. However, cracks began to form during the second year. Dick was just not behaving appropriately, and Nikki told him so. In fact, the way Nikki put it, the poor man couldn't do anything right. He didn't spend enough time with the kids, but he also didn't spend enough time with her. He didn't do enough around the house, yet at the same time he didn't do enough fun stuff. Nikki complained about finances but also complained if he worked overtime. It seemed like whatever Dick did wasn't good enough.

By the second year together, Nikki's Judge was alive and active. Her judgments of Dick were searing. And although she said he didn't seem to respond, he apparently was absorbing all the scolding words, because by the start of the third year of marriage, he was all but gone. Nikki eventually found out that Dick was having an affair. They broke up and Nikki was devastated. She felt like she had been lied to for years. Unfortunately, she had. But who the real liar was may surprise you.

In 2000, Bartels and Zeki, at the University College London, reported that fMRI studies of people in love showed massive deactivation in the individual's right hemisphere.[205] In other words, when you fall in love, you're almost entirely operating from your left hemisphere.* This is significant because your left hemisphere does something your right hemisphere wouldn't even (pardon the pun) think of doing—your left hemisphere fibs. That's right, that sweet, innocent-looking lump of gray matter is a pants-on-fire liar.

In his book *The Tell-Tale Brain*, neuroscientist V. S. Ramachandran explains that the left hemisphere is egocentric and focused on self. Not only is it fixated on what it likes, it also wants to look good. It's so concerned with how it's perceived that it might make up things to

---

*They found deactivation of the right prefrontal, parietal, and middle temporal cortex; also the posterior cingulate gyrus and medial prefrontal cortex.

preserve harmony and the overall view of itself. This wild concocting of tall tales is a process Ramachandran calls "confabulation."[206] This is almost like lying, except it can be done without conscious intent. In other words, your left hemisphere has been known to tell a fish story if it will make itself look better, and you might not even be aware of it.

This means that for those last couple of years, you've been living in a true fantasyland. Not only could you not see clearly, your own brain has been lying to you.

## WHY?
## FALLING OUT OF FALLING IN LOVE

Why does Mother Nature do all this to you? Why would she shut down important parts of your brain while making you obsessed? Why would she make your own brain lie to you? And why, after engineering all this, would she stop?

Love is about making yourself vulnerable to another person. This goes against your own nature. Being vulnerable is risky. Therefore, you naturally become protective of yourself. This protection can prevent you from finding love. Therefore, Mother Nature gives you a little assist by manipulating your brain.

However, that neurological shake-up you experienced when you fell in love can't last. Eventually your brain needs to return to homeostasis, or the state of relative stability. You can't walk around obsessed with your beloved indefinitely; you wouldn't get anything done. If your serotonin level stayed low, you would sink into depression. And if your cortisol level stayed high, it would depress your immune system, which would make you more susceptible to diseases like cancer. As wonderful as falling in love is, I'm afraid it must end. But its ending is really about real love.

When I was a little girl, my father bought me a hot pink Schwinn girl's bicycle. It had a long banana seat with bright flowers, a basket, and pink tassels that flowed off the handgrips and fluttered in the wind. Once I saw my shiny brand-new bike, that old plastic Big Wheel became a distant memory. This was the big time, but I wasn't really ready for it yet, so my dad added training wheels. I loved that bike and rode it every day. But with the training wheels on, I still felt like a little kid. I wanted to grow up, so I pestered my dad to remove the little wheels. Finally, the day came. I had arrived in Big Girlville. Those sissy baby training wheels were finally coming off.

Although I wanted the training wheels removed, a part of me still had fear. What if I fell down and hurt my bike? What if I fell down and hurt myself? Excitement and fear mixed as he stood the bike up without the little wheels. This was going to be it. I jumped on and gave my dad a reluctant smile. That's when he said, "Don't worry, stink [his term of endearment for me], I'll be right here." As I slowly started to pedal, I looked up. My dad was standing next to me, holding on to the silver loop on the back of the seat. I knew he wasn't going to let me fall.

I pedaled down the block with my dad running next to me holding me up. He stayed next to me so I could feel what the bike felt like to be balanced. On the way back, he would remove his hand but stayed near in case I started to fall, then he would put his hand back to set me upright. He did this over and over again until he was sure I knew what it felt like to have a steady bike that I could ride on my own.

Why do I mention this story? Because that's what Mother Nature does when you fall in love. She's showing you what love feels like. Like my dad running next to me, she's holding you in position until you get your balance.

You know what white-hot, got-to-have-it passion feels like. You now know that love is about closeness and understanding. Love is about seeing the other person in the best possible light. She shows you how to lovingly talk to each other and sometimes even helps you pick out cute little names like "sweetie pie" and "snookums."

This is the love that happens when Mother Nature breaks down your resistance long enough for you to get close to another person. When you fall in love, Mother Nature makes you artificially vulnerable to the other person. You're vulnerable, but because your alarm system is off-line, it doesn't feel like it. She's showing you that love trusts.

She lets you know that love is not supposed to judge. She shows you how to adore someone, how to be kind and caring. She holds you in this glorious, euphoric state until you know what real love is.

However, Mother Nature can't leave you like some brain-damaged, love-struck sufferer, unable to concentrate on the simplest tasks. She doesn't want to leave you wandering aimlessly, picking flowers and dreamily thinking of the moment when you can be with your beloved again. She doesn't want you to be so distracted that you will walk out into traffic or go flower picking in a bear's territory. Like a loving mother, she slowly returns your fully functional brain so that you can properly manage your life. It's as if once you have your balance, like my loving father, she lets go. Now that you know what love is supposed to feel like, she sets you free to love on your own.

## A HIGHER LOVE

Now that you have full functioning of your brain back, you have two choices. You can end the relationship or you can move into real love. If you choose to move into real love, the neural activity will begin to shift. When you fell in love, the majority of your brain activity was in your reward center, the part of your brain concerned with what feels good. When something feels good, you naturally want to do it again. When something feels bad, or takes more effort than is believed to achieve the perceived reward, you can lose incentive and the behavior ceases. This type of system is more selfish, focusing on the more immediate and the individual versus the bigger, longer-term picture.

If you choose to continue, everything changes. Shifting into a new type of love, your neural activity moves into the more evolved region of your brain. Researchers at Stony Brook University looked at fMRIs of individuals in long-term love. Unlike early love, where there was deactivation in the cortex, long-term love now shows activity in this part of the brain. In fact, they found significant activation in part of the orbitofrontal cortex.[207] This is the part of the brain involved in decision making. Here love now turns from a crazy emotion that hijacked your brain to a choice that you get to make. In the beginning, men chase and women choose. Now both choose.

*Love starts as a feeling and then becomes a choice.*

But it's not just a decision based on what feels good. This is a decision based on principles. The neural activity has moved into the region of the brain that houses more noble qualities. This type of love shares space with other giving types of love, such as parental and unconditional love. The Stony Brook researchers found that

long-term love showed common neural activity with that of maternal love.[208] And a study out of France found commonality between
long-term romantic love and unconditional love.[209] These types of
love give without expectation of reciprocation. Real love becomes
less concerned with me and more concerned with we.

Real love activates parts of the brain concerned with honorable
thoughts like morals. The orbital and medial sectors of the prefrontal
cortex, which are active in real love, have been found to play a central
role in moral appraisals.[210] Now you choose to love and live based on
ethics, principles, and what you believe to be the right thing to do.
In a sense, this shift makes real love a higher love.

A study out of Japan looked at the brain areas associated with
human virtue, specifically, for something they called "moral beauty."
Moral beauty is the emotion elicited by others' acts of virtue. When
people observe others' virtuous, commendable acts, they feel a warm,
pleasant, and "tingling" feeling. This feeling in turn can motivate
them to help others and to become better people themselves. They
describe this feeling as being "elevated." In other words, you feel
lifted and lighter when you perceive virtues.

The study produced several interesting findings. Moral judgment
starts by recruiting both the Judge and the amygdala. This would be
expected because you're deciding if what you're looking at is moral
or immoral. However, it's what happens next that's significant.

If an act, word, or deed is judged as immoral, it then activates the
superior temporal sulcus, or the "theory of mind" area. When you
consider something as immoral, you process it as being different
from yourself.

In contrast, if an act, word, or deed is judged as moral, it takes
a different route. A moral act or moral beauty activates regions

associated with positive emotions, like the orbitofrontal cortex.[211] This is the area of the brain that houses kindness and understanding, the same area activated by real love.

This makes real love a more empathetic and compassionate type of love. To test this theory, researchers in Sweden asked Tibetan Buddhists to participate in compassion meditation, a technique that generates feelings of compassion and benevolence. While the Buddhists meditated, the researchers conducted fMRIs on them to determine which part of their brains became active. The researchers found that focusing on compassion activated the medial prefrontal cortex.[212] This confirmed that love and compassion activate the same area of your brain, which suggests that when you initiate one, the other naturally follows.

This new love is changing and evolving. This is a greater love, a more noble, principled, and caring love. It's not a crazy, obsessed feeling, but now it's a grand decision that you make based on morals and virtues.

## REAL LOVE IS PROTECTIVE

This neural area where love now lives can help a relationship last a lifetime. To test if this new location helps relationships last, researchers at the University of California and eHarmony (the dating site) researchers set out to determine if real love helped people stay committed. They wanted to test if real love engages cognitive mechanisms associated with the preservation of the relationship. In other words, when you think about your beloved, would those thoughts help you to avoid the temptation to cheat?

In the study, an attractive other was presented to the participants.

Next, the researchers focused the participants' emotions by having them write about love. To encourage sexual desire for their partner, one group wrote about that. Another group had a random writing assignment. The researchers then measured how many times the participants thought about the attractive other to find out if activating love by writing about it helped suppress the thoughts of the attractive alternative and the potential to cheat.

The results confirmed what the researchers suspected—love did suppress thoughts of attractive others. They didn't find the same results for sexual desire with those who participated in the random writing assignment, which suggests that the quashing effect is specific to love. In fact, the stronger the participants' commitment to their partner, the less they thought or remembered the attractive other.[213] It looks like this type of love has a protective effect that helps preserve the relationship.

However, this protective effect differs from individual to individual. This part of the brain is also involved in something called "executive functioning" or "cognitive control." People have differing degrees of cognitive control. Greater activity in the orbitofrontal cortex usually means greater cognitive control. It's this cognitive control that protects the relationship. A study from the Netherlands found that romantically involved people with a higher level of cognitive control experience less difficulty staying faithful. The researchers found that individuals with greater cognitive control showed less relationship-threatening behavior, like flirting, and have a greater tendency to keep themselves out of situations where they will be tempted.[214] In other words, the more active the part of your brain that houses love is, the less likely you are to put your relationship in harm's way. The stronger, more principled, and less impulsive someone is, the more likely they are to have a strong relationship. Not only is this a love that can last a lifetime, it appears it can also make your life last longer.

## BENEFITS OF HAPPY, LONG-TERM RELATIONSHIPS

A study out of Japan showed that love could make you healthier. In the study researchers found that the sight of a loved one can induce natural killer cells (NK) in some people.[215] Natural killer cells are immune system cells that fight viruses, bacteria, and tumor cells. An increase in natural killer cells can protect you against infection.

An improved immune system might be one reason that married people, on average, enjoy better mental and physical health than unmarried people. One study found that nonmarried women had a 50 percent greater death rate, while men had a 250 percent greater death rate.[216]

Research also suggests that love can have a protective effect against addiction. For example, researchers at the Perelman School of Medicine at the University of Pennsylvania found that rats that showed a slower response to self-administered cocaine, an indication that rewarding effects of cocaine were decreased, had a higher level of brain-derived neurotropic factor (BDNF), which blunts the behavioral effects of cocaine.[217] BDNF increases when you fall in love.

Love also makes you more stable. Psychologists at the German universities of Jena and Kassel discovered that a loving, romantic relationship has a positive effect on one's personality. They followed 245 couples for nine months, interviewing them every three months over the course of their relationship. What they found was that a loving relationship had a stabilizing effect. Even people who were anxious, insecure, easily annoyed, depressed, and who had a low self-esteem and a general dissatisfaction with life showed positive improvements when in a loving relationship.[218]

Functional MRIs of long-term romantic love found recruitment of opioid and serotonin-rich neural regions. These systems have the capacity to modulate anxiety and pain. They are also the brain regions targeted for treatment of anxiety, obsessive-compulsive disorder, and depression.[219] When you fall in love, your serotonin level drops in order to promote partner obsession. But now, in an ironic twist, long-term love is protective, guards against obsession, and safeguards you from depression and anxiety.

The benefits of long-term happy relationships are numerous. Relationship satisfaction predicts global happiness, above and beyond other types of satisfaction.[220] In other words, it appears that the true key to happiness is a happy relationship. A happy long-term relationship also predicts psychological well-being and physical health, and may help buffer stressful life events.[221] In other words, if you guard against stress in your relationship, your relationship will guard you from stress.

But the true purpose for real love might be much more than this. Real love is about growing and evolving as a human being. Some believe love is about self-expansion.

## SELF-EXPANSION

Arthur Aron, a professor at Stony Brook University, proposes that the true purpose of romantic relationships is self-expansion. The self-expansion model is a theory that humans have a yearning to grow and develop. This is what motivates people to try new, exciting, and challenging activities. It's also one of the reasons you tend to be attracted to people with opposite characteristics. If you fall in love with someone just like you, there is no real growth. However, if you fall in love with someone who's different from you, you're exposed to new ideas and beliefs.

You also get to grow by learning acceptance and inclusion. Your partner may have ideas that don't fit with yours. Maybe he has a political view that you don't like. Your willingness to continue to be loving despite your differences softens you. Those hard lines that separated you from everyone else begin to blur. This inclusion of "others into self" creates an interconnectedness of self and others. This is believed to be the key to intimacy and the key to healing. Aron believes it has two dimensions, one of behaving close and one of feeling close.[222]

When you behave close, or in a loving manner, you choose to get past your own natural defenses. This can be scary at first, but also liberating. When you choose to be loving, you keep the neural activity in your more evolved brain instead of shrinking back into your primitive brain. This allows your brain to continue to expand.

When you fall in love, your brain produces BDNF and NGF. These act like fertilizer for your brain, growing new neurons and making new connections. Researchers in a study conducted in the Netherlands found that love broadened a participants' perceptual scope and led to increased performance on creativity tasks.[223] When you're in love, you tap into new areas of your brain and have new ideas and a sense of new opportunities. This supports the idea that falling in love is about self-expansion. You become more than you were as a single person. Now that you are two, you have more resources, more talents, and more brainpower.

BDNF helped you get past your natural defenses and avoidance behaviors to get closer to your beloved.[224] Unfortunately, now those levels have returned to normal. This means your defenses can come back. It's now up to you to continue to keep your defenses low and stay close to your partner. You've been together long enough that it shouldn't be a problem. But fear can easily bring those once-at-bay defense mechanisms to the forefront, creating a distance where there wasn't one.

It happened to me. Ed wanted to give me a treat. His ex-wife and daughters used to love going to the hair salon to be pampered and fussed over. They relished the massaging shampoo, the excitement of picking a new style, and the splendor of the indulgence.

One day as I was standing at the mirror doing my hair, Ed came up from behind me and gently wrapped his arms around my waist and put his chin on my shoulder. As he nuzzled me, he looked at me in the mirror and said, "How would you like to get your hair done, my treat?" Then he gave me a big smile that said he was sure I would love his gift. But instead of being delighted, I was devastated. I looked at his face, then to my own stringy, unworthy, spilt-ended mane, and my mind screamed, "He doesn't like your hair." My mind, which was trying to protect me, jumped to a crazy conclusion. I pulled back and asked, "What's wrong with my hair?"

You should've seen that poor man's face—the shock in the moment when good intentions meet bad internal voices. His hands dropped from around my waist as he backed up in horror. He backpedaled hard, saying, "No, no. Your hair looks great. Never mind." Then he made a quick exit.

## STRESS

Your reactivated brain can wreak havoc. Once your amygdala, judge, and defenses return, they can cause stress and drama. The problem is, little stresses can build up over time and have a devastating effect on your relationship.

In a joint study from Germany, Italy, and Switzerland, researchers found that stress was not perceived as a reason for divorce. However, when considering everyday stresses, participants reported trivial daily events to be one of the main reasons that contributed to their decision to divorce. The participants considered the accumulation of everyday stresses as a central trigger to divorce.[225] In other words, when the couples were asked if stress directly caused their divorce, they said "no." But after they took a closer look at all the factors, they realized it wasn't one big stressful thing but rather a buildup of little stressors over time. This makes stress potentially the number one enemy of love.

Stress, even moderate stress, has been found to have major effects on your brain. Not only does it trigger your amygdala, it can cause the amygdala to increase in size.[226] The stress of your amygdala coming back online can actually cause the amygdala to expand, creating more potential for stress. Just like the positive feedback loop where oxytocin causes more cuddling, which releases more oxytocin, which causes more loving, the amygdala has a feedback loop too. Here stress causes the amygdala to fire, which produces more stress, which causes the amygdala to fire more. Like a muscle, the more you use the amygdala, the larger it grows. This in turn makes it more sensitive to stress and more likely to be triggered.

At the same time, stress can shrink the hippocampus and prefrontal cortex, decreasing their efficiency.[227] This can change your behavior and outlook. For example, low self-esteem in humans has been associated with a smaller hippocampus, while impulsiveness and poor executive function have been associated with a defective prefrontal cortex.[228]

In a Yale University study, researchers found that changes during stress can rapidly switch off prefrontal function. Their work showed that neurons in the prefrontal cortex disconnect and stop firing after being exposed to a flood of stress hormones.[229] Your prefrontal cortex is the part of your brain that governs decision making. It can be considered the voice of reason. Without it, you can now be at the whim of your less civilized and more impulsive primitive brain. This can make you more vulnerable to urges like eating (particularly fatty or sugary foods) and impulsive and risky behaviors, like gambling, flirting, anger, and fighting to win.

> *Stress can make you more vulnerable to things like outside attention, anger, overeating, and disengaging.*

The prefrontal cortex is not as strong as the primitive area of the brain. In fact, the first hint of danger and an automatic override occurs when the instincts of the primitive brain short-circuit the prefrontal cortex. This can make the process of true love precarious.

The more primitive part of your brain is concerned with survival. Without the prefrontal cortex moderating your responses, it can feel like every stress is a matter of life or death. Simple disagreements can escalate. Sometimes almost overnight your sweet union melts, leaving two individuals in their separate corners fighting over whose perception is right.

## BREAKUPS

Sometimes the stress builds up or the defenses are so strong that the relationship breaks up. But that's okay. A breakup can be part of your happily ever after. What? Did I say that right? Happily ever after the breakup? How can it be happily ever after if you broke up? Because love is still a process, one of personal growth. It's a process of breaking down your natural defenses to become vulnerable to another person. It's a process of becoming better than you were and developing your higher self. It's a process of learning to love.

Since love is about personal growth, sometimes you need to break out of the relationship you're in, in order to grow further, often in another. Remember Nikki, who complained about her husband until the marriage collapsed? Sometimes we need to lose a relationship so we can grow. Eventually Nikki will get to the point where she stops looking at and blaming Dick. When that time comes, she'll have to take a close look at herself. She'll have to do some self-reflection. She'll need to own up that at the time she married her husband, she was in love with him, but over time she felt that she had made a bad partner choice. She'll see that she didn't respect him, and this came out in little barbs and insults. Eventually, her contempt pushed him away.

This concept is something that famed researcher Dr. John Gottman of the Gottman Institute calls "the Four Horsemen" (as in the four horsemen of the apocalypse). When these show up, Gottman predicts that a couple is heading for divorce. The Four Horseman are criticism, defensiveness, contempt, and stonewalling. Stonewalling is when the listener withdraws from interacting.[230]

Once a relationship erodes to this level, it's not healthy for anyone. Some couples can work on the relationship to enhance communication and bring them close again. But for some, like Nikki, the best course of action is to split and reevaluate.

Nikki believed the issue was all Dick's problem. But the truth is, it could've been any Tom, Dick, or Harry. The real issue is Nikki's. For a brief moment, when she and Dick fell in love, she became vulnerable and loving. However, when love became real, her defenses and fear returned.

Nikki's problem wasn't Dick but her own past. Nikki's mother died when she was seven years old. This was an extremely painful time in her life, but she never really got a chance to grieve because Nikki's father remarried quickly and expected her to act like everything was fine. Unfortunately, underneath it all, Nikki still had a lot of hurt and fear. Earlier I noted that part of your temporal lobe, the area that's known to house negative memories, goes dim when you fall in love. Once you get past the initial, crazy stage of love and are in a healthy relationship, this part fires up again and memories return. Ideally, now that you're with a partner, you can process these painful memories and heal. However, for some people, like Nikki, the pain is unfortunately turned toward the partner.

Nikki's divorce was one end of the spectrum. At the other end was Kelly. Kelly and John were married for six years. They had two beautiful children, a great house, and jobs they both liked. However, by the end of the fifth year of marriage, they just felt like they had grown apart. There was no stress or disagreements. They had grown as people, but felt they couldn't grow any further in the relationship.

In a joint study with universities in New York and China, researchers looked at couples as they progressed in their relationship. They studied couples who had fallen in love, then followed up with them eighteen months later. The couples at follow-up who reported higher relationship happiness had activity in their superior frontal gyrus.[231] The superior frontal gyrus is the part of the brain that's involved in self-awareness and introspection.[232] It helps you figure out how you feel about things. Now you're more self-aware, more conscious, and more introspective. You're no longer on autopilot and are making decisions with clarity. The people who moved out of the subconscious autopilot of love and actually took a deeper look at themselves were the happiest.

Kelly and John's divorce was amicable. A few years later they both remarried other people. When they looked back, they felt they had tried to live a life they were supposed to, not what they wanted to. When they broke apart, they figured out what they really wanted and what was important. Their next relationships were very different from the first.

Both of these divorce scenarios, Kelly and John and Nikki and Dick, are still part of the theory that love and relationships are about growing as an individual. In an ideal world, each person would grow in the relationship. Unfortunately, for some people to grow, they may need to break away to be able to take a look at themselves. Some need to deal with their past and heal, others need emotional development, and a few just need to figure out what they really want from life. The beauty is that when the relationship ends, they are now free to start the process again. Some are lucky enough to gain a perspective and start over with the same person, while others need to fall in love with someone else. If a current relationship is stagnant or not aiding one's growth, breaking away and falling in love again with a new person can enhance neuroplasticity, improve self-esteem, and promote greater empathy.

*Sometimes you must break apart for your own growth.*

I mention breakups because I want you to know that no relationship fails. Some end, but they don't fail. The only failure when it comes to love is not trying. When you get so scared of getting hurt that you protect yourself from being vulnerable, that's when you fail. But if you're willing to love, you never fail.

The willingness to be vulnerable and loving is quite rare. So rare, that if you master it, you will never be alone. You will have a line of people at your door looking for what you have to offer.

In this chapter, I explained what happens to you once love gets real. I mentioned the part about breakups, because unfortunately, some couples do break up. But the good news is that you don't have to. I told you in the beginning of the book that you now hold the keys to a happy relationship. In Chapter 9, I'll explain how you can master the secrets of happily ever after.

# CHAPTER

# THE TRUTH ABOUT
# HAPPILY EVER AFTER

Dr. George Vaillant of Harvard Medical School believes that love is in a group called "positive emotions." These emotions include love, hope, joy, forgiveness, compassion, trust, gratitude, and awe. Charles Darwin called these social emotions; they help us "to break out of the ego of I and mine." They are more about "us" than "me." You don't have to be taught; rather, you're hardwired to produce them.[233]

In Chapter 8, you learned that love, compassion, and empathy are connected. By practicing one, you can trigger the others. It also holds true for positive emotions. By practicing one, the others follow. For example, if you want to feel more love with your partner, you can start by practicing gratitude. If you want more joy in the relationship, practice forgiveness, and if you want more hope for the future, practice trust.

Vaillant refers to these emotions as being part of "emotional spirituality." He believes that it's the practice of these emotions that has helped us to evolve from selfish reptiles to loving, playful, passionate mammals to reflective, cause-seeking Homo sapiens.[234] By finding and then choosing to be loving, you become a better person. You move from a selfish, self-seeking individual to a caring, compassionate couple.

## THE PRACTICE

Once you're in a committed relationship and have fallen in love, you now find yourself on the other side. What you do next can either help you have lifelong love or send you on another search. Love now becomes a choice. When you first fell in love, it was a feeling; here, love becomes something you practice.

The key is remembering what you learned when you first fell in love. When you first fell in love, Mother Nature showed you what love looks like. Now, like my loving father holding my bike, she knows you know, so she's letting you go. How far you go is up to you. Here is where you need to apply what you've learned.

When you first fell in love, you learned that love trusts, doesn't judge, is exciting, gives, and looks at the best in your partner. To achieve happily ever after, you now need to start practicing these, even when you don't feel like it. This love becomes more concerned about giving love than getting it. But, ironically, by giving love, you receive love.

Holly found herself withdrawing more and more in the relationship. When I asked her why, she said, "Because he's being a jerk."

Then I asked, "So why did you pull back?"

"I guess I was waiting for him to come and apologize," she answered.

"Did he apologize?" I asked.

"No, it seemed to get worse."

Pulling back or withdrawing is a common pattern in relationships. The idea is that you pull away and the other person realizes that you've pulled away, and because they love you so much, they come running to see what's wrong.

This type of response works great when you're in the obsessive phase of falling in love. But once the obsession is over, this doesn't work anymore. In fact, now it can have an unintended opposite effect.

Someone's having a bad day and reacts poorly, causing the other person to feel threatened and defensive. That person goes off by himself or herself or maybe talks with a friend. Animosity builds and the gap widens. Each waits for the other to be the first person to apologize or reengage. Sometimes the next interaction is also negative, causing more hurt feelings and more withdrawal. The next thing you know, the house has grown cold and both people are unhappy. The reason this can happen so easily is because love itself is a type of feedback loop.

## THE LOVE FEEDBACK LOOP

Research psychologist Bianca Acevedo performed fMRI brains scans on couples who had been together for an average of four years. She found heightened activity in the part of the brain said to contain the mirror neuron system.[235] The mirror neuron system is what allows us to evolve so quickly. Instead of learning how to do something from trial and error, I simply need to watch you with my mirror neurons to understand how to do it.

As neuroscientist V. S. Ramachandran explains, "When you watch someone else reach for a glass of water, your mirror neurons automatically simulate the same action in your (usually subconscious) imagination."[236] In other words, merely watching another person do something or act a certain way affects your brain, as though you just did it yourself, and you don't even know it. This is the reason why athletes watch highlight videos and why love stories make us feel so good. Our mirror neurons make it feel like we are doing it.

So when you practice love, you feel it, but the other person will also feel it, as if they were doing it themselves. And because it already feels like they are practicing love, they are more likely to practice love themselves. In a way, you're training them to be more loving. Conversely, if you're acting petty or aggressive, you're stimulating that response in the other person. This is one of the reasons why hostage negotiators are so calm and compassionate. They want the perpetrator to calm down, think about his or her actions, and feel some benevolence.

This is also why you want to be more caring and loving in your relationship. Whatever action you do, the other person feels and does. With mirror neurons, love becomes self-amplifying. When your partner feels and learns more love, he or she mirrors more love back to you.

## PRACTICE ADMIRATION

When you fell in love, without the critical verdicts of your Judge, you viewed your beloved as the greatest, most amazing creature that ever graced this planet. Your love grew as your beloved basked in your admiration. Therefore, it should be of no surprise to discover that one of the biggest predictors of relationship longevity and happiness is one's ability to maintain those feelings.

In a survey of 470 studies on compatibility, psychologist Marcel Zentner of the University of Geneva found no particular combination of personality traits that lead to sustained romance, with the expectation of one: the ability to sustain "positive illusions" of one's partner.[237] Couples who continue to admire the qualities that attracted them to each other in the first place experience long-term happiness. This means that a couple can "think" their way into happiness. When you still see your beloved as funny, cute, or exciting, it keeps them funny, cute, and exciting, helping to keep the passion alive.

*Mutual admiration is a key to long-term love.*

This is true for both men and woman. In one study, a random sample of 274 U.S. married individuals found that 40 percent of those married more than ten years reported being "very intensely in love." One of the biggest predictors of that intensity of love for a man was thinking positively about his partner.[238] Another study at the Ontario Science Center in Toronto, Ontario, found that a woman's idealism about her mate consistently predicted greater relationship longevity.[239] When you look for the best in your partner, you both win.

What does having "positive illusions" mean? Does it mean you have to be amazing or perfect for your partner to think you are? Surprisingly, no. In fact, researchers have found that perceiving a fallible partner heightens tendencies toward idealization.[240] This means that you and your partner don't have to be the most beautiful, funniest, exciting, or the best at anything. The more human and authentic you are, the greater the chance that your partner will think you're the most beautiful, funniest, exciting, or the best. Conversely, the more quirky or imperfect your beloved is, the greater you will probably adore them. With positive illusions, you'll think they're perfect. That's the point of illusions—they don't have to be based in facts. In fact, John Holmes of the University of Waterloo found that positive illusions seem to have surprisingly little grounding in interpersonal realities, suggesting that idealism is in part unwarranted.[241]

Carol likes to tell the story about how she met Gary on the subway in Manhattan. "I was reading a book, so at first I didn't notice him," she says. "Then he sat down next to me and made a joke about the book I was reading. He made me laugh. That was twenty-six years ago, and he's still fun to be with. He makes me laugh almost every day," she added.

But it's not necessarily the words that Carol speaks that are important when she tells that story. Rather it's what happens to Carol when talks about Gary. Her face changes and her eyes become more distant. It's as if she's watching her own movie in her mind's eye. She's flashing back on all those fun times, all those jokes and laughter. Carol chooses to focus on the part she loves about Gary, his sense of humor. Gary's not a stand-up comedian, and I'm sure not every day is fun. But in Carol's mind, he's the greatest. And that's all that really matters.

When your inner Judge returns, you have a choice. You can listen to the new, unfavorable critiques that arise or you can choose to dismiss those and focus on the parts you like. You're moving from an automatic feeling to a choice. What you choose now dictates what you feel. In fact, researchers have found that individuals reported greater satisfaction, trust, and love, and less ambivalence and conflict, the greater their partner's idealism.[242] You can focus on the positive attributes of your partner and your relationship, and your relationship will be positive, or you can focus on the negative and get more of that.

When you first fall in love, you're convinced that you've met "the one," the perfect person for you. However, as your full brain function returns, little doubts surface. If you allow those uncertainties to grow, they will erode your loving relationship over time. Therefore, it's probably not surprising that researchers have found that a sense of conviction or security in your relationship creates stronger and happier relationships. Researchers have also discovered that people believed their own relationships were relatively immune to the dangers of their partners' attributes. This gave them seemingly exaggerated feelings of control, and considerable optimism for the future.[243] Therefore, if you want a happily-ever-after future, it helps to maintain the memories of the illusions from the past.

## PRACTICE GIVING AND FORGIVING

The more you give love, the more your partner feels. This in turn builds their trust, love, and security in the relationship. It also relieves their doubts, thereby strengthening their conviction. This in turn will help build your trust, because their strong conviction decreases your doubts; and *because* you know you can trust them, it increases their love, because they feel loved and are less afraid to love.

It's tempting to pull back when you're upset. The theory is that your partner will see your distress and show that they love you by coming to your aid. This theory worked great when you fell in love. Then, your beloved was so obsessed with you that the slightest hint that you might be moving away would have him pouncing like a dog on a ball.

> *Pulling back no longer works in real love.*

Now that the obsessive phase is over, you need a new plan. If you pull back, their mirror neurons pick that up and they learn to pull back also. Therefore, you pull back, hoping for them to come to you, but they see you pulling away and they mirror your response by pulling back themselves. You respond by pulling further back, and the next thing you know your hot passion is turning cold and your oxytocin is dropping. This makes you less likely to touch, kiss, or cuddle. Now you're losing the oxytocin feedback loop, and you're feeling less loved.

When a man feels that his beloved is pulling back, his response is often to focus on something else. He spends more time at work or on a hobby to keep his mind off the approaching cold front. And the next thing they know, they're living on separate ends of an iceberg, wondering what happened to the love.

So how do you move from the ice age to global warming? By practicing giving. Instead of withdrawing and waiting for your partner to ask what's wrong, go talk to them. Remember, you have now moved to a more mature love. For example, say something like, "When you said my hair looked flat, I heard you didn't think it looked good. Is that what you meant?" Now, either he'll say, "Yes, I like your hair curlier," or "No, I was just making an observation." Many times what you hear and what a person meant are two different things.

Once the issue is out, now you can practice giving. This may sound trite, but I'll be the first to admit that it's not easy. When I first tried to practice this with Ed, I found it hard. When I felt upset, I would naturally withdraw and often call a friend. In the past, I would call a friend who would support me and commiserate. They would take my side and support my childish response. This, of course, didn't help my relationship.

This time, I got a mentor. Instead of telling me I was right, she would remind me to be kind. I was reminded that many times a fight or a withdrawal is a plea for love. When we don't feel love, we pull back. The answer is not to meet their pulling back with more of the same. Rather, the answer is to coax the person back with love.

Once I told her my position, she would say, "Okay, that's fine; now go and ask him if he would like a cup of tea." The first time she suggested this, I almost chipped a tooth with my defensive jaw clenching. My mind screamed, *No way; he has to come to me.* I told my mentor, "Yeah, but he's being a jerk." She responded with "Yes, I know, but do you want to be right, or do you want to be happy?" In other words, is this the hill I want the relationship to die on? When you choose to be right, it automatically makes the other person wrong. Making Ed feel like he's in the wrong lowers his testosterone, so he'll fight to prevent that. Next thing we know, we're both defending ourselves and no one wins.

At this point in my life, I became willing to set down my pettiness and the need to be right for the higher goal of a loving relationship. Therefore, I went back into the room with Ed. As I entered the room, I could see his body tighten like he was bracing for a fight. I walked up to him and asked, "Would you like a cup of tea?" His response was surprised; he paused for a moment and then said "sure."

I walked back in a few minutes later with a hot cup of tea and handed it to him. At first he looked at it with suspicion. I think he even sniffed it, maybe to smell for poison. Then he relaxed and the tension drained from his shoulders. Once we both lowered our defenses, we were able to talk like two people who actually love each other.

Since that time, there have been other occasions when we've become defensive. However, with enough practice, we can snap out of it by reminding each other that we're on the same team. That is to say, we love each other and want this relationship.

I had a client call who was very distressed. She loved her husband but said he was driving her crazy.

"I just don't understand it. He forgets everything," she said.

"What's been going on?"

"I have to remind him ten times that we have an engagement. I had been telling him for weeks that we had my cousin's birthday party coming up and that he needed to pick up the balloons. Last night when he came home from work, do you think he had the balloons?" she asked.

"My guess would be no," I said.

"Yeah, and to make matters worse, he forgot, showed up late, and we ended up late for the party because we had to make a special trip for the balloons. I love him, but sometimes I could kill him," she said.

I hear this complaint about men forgetting all the time. Women are much better at remembering because of that larger hippocampus I mentioned in Chapter 2. Not only that, when a man falls in love, his drop in testosterone affects his hippocampus, causing it to shrink. So not only has the poor guy given up some strength, drive, and stamina to be with you, he probably has given up some of his ability to remember, as well as some of his internal GPS. Therefore, if you notice that your guy forgets more than usual, or seems to get lost, just remember: this was his sacrifice for loving you.

I've talked about the importance of practicing the things you learned when you fell in love. However, the real secret to happily ever after may come down to the care and maintenance of three important neurotransmitters.

## BOMBPROOF YOUR RELATIONSHIP

In a recent study of 437 divorcing men and women, one of the main factors cited for the divorce was unmet emotional needs.[244] But how do you know what the emotional needs of your partner are? And how do you know if you're meeting them? Often you do what you think you would want done. That would be great if your partner was a carbon copy of you, but they are not. Men and women are different; therefore each one has different needs. In addition, there are lots of different types of needs. How do you know which ones are important?

To bombproof your relationship, that is, protect it from being destroyed, you want to choose and practice love while meeting each other's needs. To do this you need to choose practices that help maintain three critical neurotransmitters: dopamine levels in both, her oxytocin level, and his testosterone level.

## DOPAMINE = PASSION

As a relationship ages, the excitement tends to decrease as you come to know each other. The relationship can become predictable and even routine. The passion, once burning red hot, now slowly turns tepid. However, some couples are able to maintain intense, passionate, romantic love for many years.

Researchers decided to conduct fMRIs on couples who reported being intensely, madly in love after ten years together. Not surprisingly, the researchers found significant activation in the ventral tegmental area (VTA)—the dopamine-rich, reward area of the brain. In fact, the greater the closeness the person experienced with their partner, the greater the reward response,[245] indicating they were experiencing considerable pleasure from being in the relationship.

So how did they maintain that intensity? The researchers discovered that if couples participated in new, novel, and rewarding activities, their neural activation in the VTA would continue.[246] Doing new things together like new hobbies or new adventures, such as travel and learning about new cultures, can keep the dopamine elevated. Participating in thrilling activities such as zip lining, rock climbing, or simply doing something that makes you nervous can also increase norepinephrine along with the dopamine, compounding the excitement.

This excitement factor was confirmed in another study. Researchers had couples either participate in mundane activities or challenging ones, like moving an object together without using their hands, arms, or teeth. The relationship quality was evaluated both before and after the activities, to see if participating in the exercise had any effect. The researchers found that participating in this shared novel and arousing activity helped relieve feelings of boredom and improved relationship quality.[247]

## PRACTICE WITH FRIENDS

In a joint study with the University of Colorado–Boulder and Wayne State University, researchers tested the effects spending time with other couples had on a relationship. In two different studies, the researchers looked at what effect spending time with other couples had on a person's self-disclosure. In other words, would spending time with other couples help people open up? The study found that when paired with other couples, people tended to open up more and share more intimate details about their lives.

Next, another study looked at the effect that self-disclosure had on the individual and the couples. They found that high self-disclosure interaction with other couples increased a couple's passion. The study concluded that the creation of couple friendships could be an additional way to reignite feelings of passionate love in romantic relationships.[248] The embers of passionate love are continually stoked by new and novel activities; these can include fun shared events with other couples.

## PRACTICE ALONE

For a happy, healthy relationship, you need to do things together but still have a life of your own. Being too dependent on the other person for your happiness puts an undo strain on the relationship. Yes, you need to do new and fun things together, but it's also a good idea to have your own activities that also give you pleasure.

Researcher conducted fMRIs on people to see what part of the brain passion activates. They examined both passion for a partner and general passion, such as hobbies. The researchers found that the two share some common reward circuitry.[249] This then suggests that having your own hobbies and activities that make you excited can also strengthen your relationship.

A study asked one hundred couples to name the most important factors that contributed to marital satisfaction. Women stated passionate love was important. Passionate love is the intense longing for the partner and the desire to be close. Where passionate love is, oxytocin is sure to follow. However, the study found that for men, passionate love was not the most important factor.[250] So if you're a woman trying to build a connection with your man, cuddling and talking alone are not going to do it. You want to keep the passion alive, but even more important, you want to pay attention to his testosterone level.

## HIS TESTOSTERONE

When a man commits, his testosterone drops. Unfortunately, low testosterone is associated with lethargy and depression. On the other hand, as an Air Force study found, high testosterone is found in men as they are contemplating divorce.[251] This is usually caused by conflict and fighting at home.

Therefore, for a man to be truly happy and content in a relationship, his testosterone needs to be not too high and not too low. You want his testosterone to be just right, and stay in the testosterone sweet spot.

Prior to Nikki and Dick's divorce, Nikki had lost respect for Dick. His poor handling of their finances upset her. She began to hurl thinly veiled insults at him in the form of snide comments. She would say things like, "You can't do anything right." Dick also had pressure at work. He wasn't winning at work or at home. His testosterone tank was probably pretty close to empty. He needed to get a "win" quick. Of course, we know what he did. He got his needed testosterone boost in the form of a new girlfriend.

## Figure 6. Testosterone Fluctuations

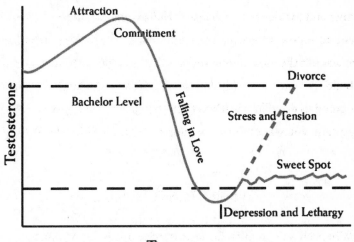

At the other end of the testosterone spectrum are couples who fight often. The stress and tension can cause a hostile environment, which raises his testosterone. His level becomes high enough and blocks all effects of oxytocin. This can lead to his withdrawal and what Gottman calls "stonewalling," without him ever leaving the house.

The main reason I wrote this book is to help empower people. One of my impetuses was a woman named Sue. Sue was part of a weekly coaching group. When I asked Sue what her main problem with relationships was, she said, "They all get lazy and turn into wimps."

She continued, "I'm a strong, independent woman; I have my own home and business. But I seem to attract weak guys. They start out all right and then something happens. I'm looking for a man who can add to my life, be my equal and tough enough to hold his own with me."

What Sue has is a great dilemma. She wants a man to stay strong and tough but also commit. Now that you understand what happens when a man falls in love, you can see the problem here. As soon as he commits, his toughness begins to soften as his testosterone drops. At the same time, as Sue falls in love, her testosterone rises. This creates a greater disparity, where she becomes even more dominant than usual. She also wants him to leave his territory and move into her home, which further weakens his dominance. Soon the masculine-feminine dynamics feel like they have switched.

In all of these cases, the usual result is the end of the relationship, or worse, years of unhappily ever after. But there are things that you can do to help keep his testosterone in the sweet spot.

## GIVE HIM A WIN

Rachel called me and said, "Brad and I aren't doing well."

"What's wrong?" I asked.

"He's just not doing anything around the house anymore. For example, last night I reminded him to take out the trash. But today he left for work and the trash was still there!" she exclaimed.

I learned that when they first moved in together, Rachel would appreciate it when Brad took out the trash. But now it's his job and she expects him to do it. In fact, if he doesn't do it in a timely manner, Rachel becomes upset and nags him. Brad hates the nagging and doesn't want to be told what to do. So, he'll do just about anything else than take out the trash.

A man's testosterone level fluctuates around a set point, increasing with "wins" and decreasing with "loses." When a man does something for you, it's a win. It makes him feel good and gives his testosterone

THE TRUTH ABOUT HAPPILY EVER AFTER


a little boost. However, when something is required, or worse, demanded, the winning effect is lost. In some cases, such as when nagging is involved, it can lower his testosterone level. As the testosterone gets lower, so does his motivation.

Now he has no other recourse than to try and get a testosterone boost. To do this, he'll need to win a challenge. When he resists taking out the trash, it gives him a "win" and supplies him with his needed lift. The problem is, to get this boost, he must compete and win against you.

A man can get a testosterone boost when he's aggressive. The form I just mentioned of avoiding taking out the trash is passive-aggressive. In fact, his testosterone-generating boost doesn't need to be outwardly aggressive. Researchers at Syracuse and Pennsylvania State Universities found that things like spelling bees, elections, criticism, competitions, and academic jousting can all help give his testosterone a nudge up. In addition, things like looking at porn, winning a game, and watching his team win also causes testosterone to rise, while losing the game or watching his team lose lowers his testosterone.[252]

When you nag, yell, or complain, it's a "lose" and lowers his testosterone and incentive. But when you compliment, praise, or appreciate him, that's a win. Rachel's solution was simple. She could ask him to take out the trash, and when he does, say, "Thank you."

As I tried to explain this idea to Rachel, she became upset.

"Why do I have to give him a win? He's a grown man; he should just take out the trash," she complained.

That's when I gently reminded her what he gave up to be with her. When Brad committed to her, his testosterone dropped. In a sense he was giving up something very valuable to be with her. His testosterone was his source of strength and vitality. For some men, testosterone can drop to castration levels. This means that in a way, he has given up the family jewels to be with her. The least she could do is recognize this and help him to maintain the little bit of testosterone he has left.

Simple things like saying thanks, being appreciative, and not having expectations can go a long way to maintaining his level in the sweet spot. Other ways men can get a needed boost are winning at video games, buying himself something new, or driving a sports car. In fact, if he happens to drive a family sedan, every time he gets into it, his testosterone level drops.[253] Therefore, those guys need even more love than most. It's also probably what's behind the classic midlife crisis sports car purchase. As a man ages, his testosterone naturally decreases, but a hot sports car can give it a boost. His purchase of a little red corvette may be his way of shoring up his dwindling supply of testosterone.

One way I try and give Ed a win is with jars. Whenever I make anything that requires me to open a jar, I bring it to him. He opens the jar, and I get to say "thank you." Other ways include looking for little things he's doing right, to encourage that behavior. Instead of complaining when he leaves clothes on the floor, I say "thank you" when I notice him picking them up.

Also, when I really want something, I may not ask directly. Sometimes being direct can be perceived as a challenge. A challenge can also boost testosterone, but not in a way that's beneficial to the relationship.

This was an issue with Sue. Sue was a mother of two and was used to barking out orders. Therefore, when the new beau came along, she treated him like one of her children—or worse, one of her employees. The choices he had were not good. Either he complied and was perceived as a wimp, or he revolted and started a power struggle. Either choice would eventually result in the death of the relationship.

Sue needed to see how she was contributing to this situation and make adjustments accordingly. Instead of commanding a man, she needed to give him an opportunity to please. Hinting that she wanted something, or something needed to be done, gives him the opportunity to put on his Superman cape and come to the rescue.

For example, I mentioned to Ed that I thought my tire was going flat. He heard this not as a demand (a loss) but as an opportunity to please (a win). He went out and checked the tire and added more air. He rechecked it again over the next couple of days to make sure it wasn't a slow leak. I gushed gratitude for getting my tire fixed, making me feel cherished, and he felt like a superhero for doing it—a win-win for both of us.

One study looked at the effect of gratitude on sixty-six couples who were in ongoing, satisfying, and committed relationships. They found that even though the relationships had ups and downs, they were reliably marked by one person's feelings of gratitude. The study concluded that everyday gratitude serves as an important relationship maintenance mechanism, acting as a booster shot to the relationship.[254]

Joe and Cathy credit their relationship longevity and happiness to a nightly ritual. When they get into bed, they tell each other three things they were grateful for that day. They say you can never go to bed angry when you have a grateful heart.

Joe and Cathy's nightly ritual also gives a nice boost to each of their neurotransmitters. As they do the gratitude list together, Cathy gets a nice boost of oxytocin, while Joe gets a shot of testosterone when he hears that Cathy is grateful, especially if she's grateful for something that reflects on him.

The reverse is also true. When a man hears complaints, blame, or disrespect, it can have a devastating effect on his testosterone. Before I realized what was happening, I would complain about things in hopes that Ed would do something about them. Unfortunately, it would have the opposite effect. When he heard a complaint, he heard he was doing something wrong. This would lower his testosterone and motivation. To make matters worse, things like complaining and blame can actually push him away.

A Japanese study looked at the neural activations of blame and praise. Their findings showed that blame and immoral acts activate the area of the brain involved in the theory of mind, or the part concerned with what's yours and what's not. In a way, to your brain, blame is considered an immoral act that's not about you, while praise, on the other hand, triggers the part of your brain associated with positive emotions and love.[255]

The findings of that study make a strong case for the augment that praising someone is more likely to bring about positive change than criticism and blame. When you put blame on someone else, the other person's mind wants to get as far away from you as possible. That's probably why people become defensive when they are blamed for something. Their brain is telling them that the fault does not lie with them. They will then defend their position, rather than accept a negative and objectionable act as being a part of themselves.

*Blame pushes a person away.*

On the other hand, when you praise, the other person feels great. And, as we learned from the dating phase, when something feels good, you want to do it again and again, like the rat pushing the lever.

> *Praise and winning are the ultimate relationship safeguards for a man.*

## HER OXYTOCIN

As a woman learns to trust a man, her oxytocin level slowly increases. This high oxytocin level bonds her to her partner. Oxytocin helps her to trust and keeps her defenses at bay.

In a study at the University of Bologna in Italy, scientists decided to test the effect that viewing a loved one had on defensive responses. Researchers studied the participants' startle response, such as the amount of blinks when exposed to a sound, the clenching of one's jaw, heart rate, and skin conductance or nervous perspiration when the person was presented with either a loved one, a neutral picture, or an unpleasant photo.

The researchers also showed study participants pictures of their parents versus a picture of their partner. What they found was that in all cases, the natural defensive response was buffered by love. In fact, the partner's love had a greater inhibition of defensiveness than even parental love.[256] In other words, when you're in love, you're naturally less defensive and closer to you partner. In fact, you're even less self-protective with your partner than with your parents.

The study found that the defense inhibition effect of love was even more profound in women.[257] A woman should naturally be at ease with her partner. She should be less defensive and more trusting. A woman's level of trust is connected to her level of oxytocin.

In Chapter 6, we learned that oxytocin and trust were intimately linked. Researchers in Switzerland wanted to test this theory. They set out to determine how oxytocin affected trust. In the study, the researchers broke the participants up into two groups. One group received intranasal oxytocin, while the other received a placebo. Next, the two groups participated in a money game. Basically, the game questioned how much money a person was willing to risk after they heard that the trustee only paid out 50 percent of the time.

The study found that in the group that received the placebo, trust and investment dropped dramatically. On the other hand, the oxytocin group kept the faith and even upped their ante. Next, the researchers conducted fMRIs on the oxytocin group to determine what effect it had on their brain. They found that oxytocin had a buffering effect on the amygdala.[258]

Unfortunately, little day-to-day stresses can have an effect on your oxytocin level. Worry and uncertainty can cause stress hormone levels to rise, which can impair oxytocin.[259] When a woman's oxytocin gets low, it can cause her to become disconnected, untrusting, suspicious, and defensive.

However, interestingly, if you trust your partner, your partner is probably more trustworthy. Couples with the strongest convictions about the partner's love and trustworthiness also rated their partner as more virtuous.[260] This would make perfect biological sense. If a person had strong convictions about their love, they would have less stress, increasing their position in the loving part of the brain, which, as we learned earlier, also houses morals and virtues. If a partner is perceived as solidly in love, they should be more virtuous and more trustworthy.

Therefore, if you doubt or snoop around on your partner, it sends a subtle message that your love may be eroding. Not only does this affect you, it can send a subtle subconscious message to him. Conversely, when you show him trust, it sends a jolt to his subconscious that he is loved. When he feels trusted and loved, his testosterone stays in the good zone.

In turn, when he feels trusted, he feels safe and is thus able to be more vulnerable and loving. When a woman feels that love, her oxytocin naturally increases. The oxytocin feedback loop works with kissing and cuddling as well as trusting. That's because love can be a buffer against stress. In humans, oxytocin inhibits stress response activity, including the release of cortisol.[261] Therefore, when a woman feels less stress and more love, her oxytocin level stays high. In turn, she feels more trust and love, causing her man's testosterone to be just right.

Oxytocin diversity is also important. When a woman has only one source for her oxytocin supply, it puts her supply at risk. If her partner is her main source, it can cause fear. If the partner leaves, he could take her precious supply of oxytocin with him. The same holds true for children. During childbirth, a woman gets a super dose of oxytocin. Every time she looks at her precious bundle, she gets another shot. It can become tempting for her to focus on the child for her source of oxytocin. Of course, the problem is that the child grows up, leaving an empty nest. If a woman's focus is solely on the child, this could be a huge loss. But if a woman has other sources of oxytocin, such as friends, a book club, hobbies, and even social media, she can weather the storm and keep a stable supply.

In addition, a woman's personal beliefs can have a big effect on oxytocin levels. Trust is enhanced by your own beliefs about the world. If you believe the world is a dangerous place, it can make trust and oxytocin hard to hold. But if you believe the world is safe and you are loved, trust and oxytocin stay high. This may be the reason that a study out of Portugal found that regular churchgoers, married people, and couples who enjoy harmonious social ties are most satisfied with their love lives. They found this to be true for both men and woman and for all ages from eighteen to ninety.[262]

# CONCLUSION

Once you fall in love, you too get to experience the magic. This is the stuff that poets, philosophers, and musicians have been writing about for centuries—a crazy, euphoric ecstasy, a place you can only hope to live in for the rest of your life, because this enchanted moment is ephemeral. But if you're brave enough, you can enter into another world, a warm, stable, and nurturing world that can provide you with a caring and trusting partner. That's what real love is all about.

As I was researching and writing this book, one question kept popping up: Why? Why does Mother Nature do this? Why does she make you instantly attracted to some people but then make you nervous and skeptical, only to remove that skepticism, and then have that skepticism return a short while later? Why does she have you fall in love at all? And once you're in love, why doesn't she just leave you there? This whole process seems so crazy and convoluted. Why?

Of course, I tend to look at everything through the lens of a biologist. Instead of looking at individual pieces, I look at the bigger evolutionary picture. For a species to evolve, each member must also evolve. Nature uses many means to evolve. One way is pressure. If two species compete for the same resource, such as food or space, one must adapt or risk perishing. That's evolution through pressure. Another way is evolution through incentive. If a species changes a little, it can open up a whole new area in which to live, such as evolving legs to walk on land.

Love may be evolution through incentive. When you choose love, you learn how to love. When you're in a loving relationship, you're happier and healthier. You learn to see and be seen, to give and to receive love. When you choose love, you become a better person. When you move past your selfish desires, you tap into a higher love, a love that shares neural connections with morals, empathy, and unconditional love. You learn to give because you learn that through giving you experience the ultimate reward—real love.

In the big picture of life, humans are the apex species. This means that what we do and the choices we make can have a direct effect on what happens to this planet. When you choose love, you become a more caring and compassionate person. You cultivate virtues and think more globally. You're less likely to make hasty decisions based on short-term, selfish desires. Rather, now you're more enlightened and likely to make decisions that not only benefit you but also others, and even, potentially, the planet as a whole.

When you practice love, you become a better person. You're more conscientious, kind, and thoughtful. This makes finding and practicing real love one of the greatest and noblest things you can do for yourself, for others, and potentially for the planet. As professor Anne Faul from the University of Louisville says, "It starts with yourself, and then it circles out into the world."[263] When you love, it affects the mirror neurons of everyone around you. In this way, when each person finds and practices love, they expand the amount of love in the world. This may be Mother Nature's ultimate goal: for all of us to find and practice love, thereby becoming a more loving planet.

Now get out there and love someone!

# ENDNOTES

1 "Study: 'Love Hormone" Roused by Social Media." Fox News Health online, www.foxnews.com/health/2012/07/12/ study-love-hormone-roused-by-social-media/#ixzz2I3mXafFt.

2 Irion, Robert. "What Proxmire's Golden Fleece Did for—and to—Science." The Scientist, Dec. 12, 1988.

3 Safire, William. Lend Me Your Ears: Great Speeches in History. New York: W. W. Norton & Co., 1992.

4 Carey, Benedict. "Watching New Love as It Sears the Brain." New York Times. May 31, 2005.

5 Kaufman, J. C., and L. A. Rosenblum. "The reaction to separation in infant monkeys: Anaclitic depression and conservation withdrawal." Psychosomatic Medicine 29 (6) (1967): 648–75.

6 Crandall, Floyd, MD. "Hospitalism." Archives of Pediatics 14(6) (June 1897): 448–54.

7 Ibid.

8 Fisher, Helen, et al. "Romantic love: A mammalian brain system for mate choice." Philos Trans R Soc Lond B Biol Sci 361(1476) (2006): 2173–86.

9 Ibid.

10 Cannon, C., and M. R. Bseikri. "Is Dopamine Required for Natural Reward?," Physiology & Behavior 81, no. 5 (July 2004): 741–48.

11  Acevedo, B., et al. "Neural correlates of long-term intense romantic love." *Social Cognitive and Affective Neuroscience* 7(2) (Feb. 2012): 149–59.

12  "Sierra Nevada Bighorn Sheep Facts." (n.d.) Retrieved November 20, 2012, from http://www.dfg.ca.gov/snbs/SheepFacts.html.

13  Iwai, N. "Morphology, function and evolution of the pseudo-thumb in the Otton frog." *Journal of Zoology* (Oct 18, 2012).

14  Slatcher, R., et al. "Testosterone and Self-Reported Dominance Interact to Influence Human Mating Behavior." *Social Psychological and Personality Science* (Feb 28, 2011).

15  Abramov, Israel, et al. "Sex & Vision I: Spatio-temporal Resolution." *Biology of Sex Differences* 3(1) (2012).

16  Gibbons, Ann. "The Brain as 'sexual organ.'" *Science* (Aug. 30, 1997): 957.

17  Panzica, G. C. "The sexually dimorphic medial preoptic nucleus of quail: A key brain area mediating steroid action on male sexual behavior." *Front Neuroendocrinol* 17(1) (Jan. 1996): 51–125.

18  Ibid.

19  Hofman, Michel, et al. "The sexually dimorphic nucleus of the preoptic area." *Journal of Anatomy* 164 (1989): 55–72.

20  Gibbons, Ann. "The Brain as 'sexual organ.'" *Science* (Aug. 30, 1997): 957.

21  Houtsmuller, E. J., et al. "SDN-POA volume, sexual behavior, and partner preference of male rats affected by perinatal treatment with ATD." *Physiol Behav* 56(3) (Sep. 1994): 535–41.

22  Xiaohang, X., et al. "Modular Genetic Control of Sexually

Dimorphic Behaviors." *Cell* 148(3) (Feb. 3, 2012): 596–607.

23 Cezario, A. F., et al. "Hypothalamic sites responding to predator threats—the role of the dorsal premammillary nucleus in the unconditioned and conditional antipredatory defensive behavior." *Eur J Neuroscience* 28(5) (Sep. 2008): 1003–15.

24 Hoeft, F., et al. "Gender Differences in the Mesocorticolimbic System During Computer Game-Play." *Journal of Psychiatric Research* 42(4) (2008): 253–258.

25 Giedd, J. N., et al. "Quantitative MRI of temporal lobe, amygdala, and hippocampus in normal human development: ages 4-18 years." *J Comp Neurol* 366 (1996): 223–30.

26 Neufang, Susanne, et al. "Sex Differences and the Impact of Steroid Hormones on the Developing Human Brain." *Cerebral Cortex* 19(2) (2009): 464–73.

27 Lee, Joohyung, and V. R. Harley. "The male fight-flight response: A result of SRY regulation of catecholamines?" *Bioessays* 34(6) (2012): 454–7.

28 Smith, E. E., and S. M. Kosslyn. *Cognitive Psychology: Mind and Brain.* Upper Saddle River, N.J.: Prentice Hall, 2007: 21, 194–199, 349.

29 Gron, G., et al. "Brain activation during human navigation: gender-different neural networks as substrate of  p e r f o r - mance." *Nature Neuroscience* 3(4) (Apr. 2000): 404.

30 Gibbons, Ann. "The Brain as 'sexual organ.'" *Science* (Aug. 30, 1997): 957.

31 Neufang, Susanne, et al. "Sex Differences and the Impact of Steroid Hormones on the Developing Human Brain." *Cerebral Cortex* 19(2) (2009): 464–73.

32 Starr, C. *Basic Concepts in Biology* 5e. Belmont, Cal.: Wadsworth Group, 2003.

33 Abramov, Israel, et al. "Sex & Vision I: Spatio-temporal Resolution." *Biology of Sex Differences* 3(1) (2012).

34 Giedd, J. N., et al. "Quantitative MRI of temporal lobe, amygdala, and hippocampus in normal human development: ages 4-18 years." *J Comp Neurol* 366 (1996): 223–30.

35 St. Jacques, Peggy, et al. "Gender differences in autobiographical memory for everyday events: Retrieval elicited by SenseCam Images vs. Verbal Cues." *Memory* 19(7) (Oct. 2011): 723–732.

36 Neufang, Susanne, et al. "Sex Differences and the Impact of Steroid Hormones on the Developing Human Brain." *Cerebral Cortex* 19(2) (2009): 464–73.

37 Greitemeyer, T., et al. "Romantic motives and risk-taking: an evolutionary approach." *Journal of Risk Research* 16(1) (2013): 19.

38 Dutton, D., and A. Aron. "Some Evidence for Heightened Sexual Attraction Under Conditions of High Anxiety." *Journal of Personality and Social Psychology* 30(4) (1974): 510–17.

39 Liston, C., et al. "Psychosocial Stress Reversibly Disrupts Prefrontal Processing and Attentional Control." *Proceedings of the National Academy of Sciences* 106(3) (2009): 912.

40 Ibid.

41 Mather, M., and N. R. Lighthall. "Both Risk and Reward Are Processed Differently in Decisions Made Under Stress." *Current Directions in Psychological Science* 21(2) (2012).

42 Loh, H., et al. "Beta-endorphin is a potent analgesic agent." *Proc Natl Acad Sci USA* 73(8) (Aug. 1976): 2895–98.

43 "Halle Berry and nine other celebrity women who are unlucky in love." *OK! Magazine*, Oct. 23, 2012.

44 Arseniuk, M. "Pamela Anderson and Tommy Lee Take Vegas Together." *Las Vegas Sun*, Aug. 2, 2009.

45 Wells, Melody S. "Pamela Anderson and Tommy Lee Back Together Again." *People*, Jun. 13, 2008. http://www.people.com/people/article/0,,20206681,00.html. Retrieved Jun. 16, 2008.

46 Simpson, J. A., et al. "The Impact of Early Interpersonal Experience on Adult Romantic Relationship Functioning: Recent Findings From the Minnesota Longitudinal Study of Risk and Adaptation." *Current Directions in Psychological Science* 20(6) (2011): 355. DOI: 10.1177/0963721411418468.

47 Bereczkei, Tamás, et al. "Sexual imprinting in human mate choice." *Proc Biol Sci* 271(1544) (Jun 7, 2004).

48 McClintock, Elizabeth. "Handsome Wants as Handsome Does: Physical Attractiveness and Gender Differences in Revealed Sexual Preferences." *Biodemography and Social Biology* 57(2) (2011): 221.

49 Bereczkei, Tamás, et al. "Sexual imprinting in human mate choice." *Proc Biol Sci* 271(1544) (Jun 7, 2004).

50 Shepher, Joseph. *Incest: A Biosocial View*. (Studies in Anthropology.) New York: Academic Press, 1983.

51 Fisher, Helen, et al. "The Neural Mechanisms of Mate Choice: A Hypothesis." *Neuroendocrinology Letters Special Issue* 23(suppl 4) (Dec. 2002).

52 Abramov, Israel, et al. "Sex & Vision I: Spatio-temporal Resolution." *Biology of Sex Differences* 3(1) (2012).

53 Holding, Cathy. "The Science of Magnetism." *The Independent*, September 12, 2008.

54 Provine, Robert R., et al. "When the Whites of the Eyes are Red: A Uniquely Human Cue." *Ethology* 117(5) (2011).

55 Buss, David, et al. "Sexual Strategies Theory: An Evolutionary Perspective on Human Mating." *Psychological Review* 100(2) (1993): 204–32.

56 Brizendine, Louann. *The Male Brain.* New York: Random House, 2010.

57 Grammer, Karl, et al. "Human pheromones and sexual attraction." *European Journal of Obstetrics & Gynecology and Reproductive Biology* 118(2) (Feb. 1, 2005): 135–142.

58 Meredith, Michael. "Human Vomeronasal Organ Function: A Critical Review of Best and Worst Cases." *Chem. Senses* 26(4) (2001): 433–445.

59 Panevich, Diana, et al. "Effects of Vomeronasal Organ Removal From Male Mice on Their Preference for and Neural Fos Responses to Female Urinary Odors." *Behavioral Neuroscience* 120(4) (Aug. 2006): 925–936.

60 Miller, Saul, et al. "Scent of a Woman: Men's Testosterone Responses of Olfactory Ovulation Cues." *Psychological Science* 21(2) (2010): 276–83.

61 Clutton-Brock, Tim. "Female Mate Choice in Mammals." *The Quarterly Review of Biology* 84(1) (2009).

62 Van Bergen, E., et al. "The scent of inbreeding a male sex pheromone betrays inbred males." *Proc Biol Sci* 280(1758) (2013).

63 Cardiff University. (2005, April 2). "Love at First . . . Smell." *ScienceDaily,* Apr. 2, 2005. www.sciencedaily.com/releases/2005/03/050326094405.htm. Retrieved Aug. 2, 2013.

64 Penn, Dustin, et al. "The Evolution of Mating Preferences

and Major Histocompatibility Complex Genes." *The American Naturalist* 153(2) (Feb. 1999).

65  Xu, Yi, et al. "Human Vocal Attractiveness as Signaled by Body Size Projection." *PLoS ONE* 8(4) (2013).

66  Smith, D. S., et al. "A modulatory effect of male voice pitch on long-term memory in women: Evidence of adaptation of mate choice?" *Memory & Cognition* 40 (2012).

67  Guéguen, N., et al. "'Love is in the air': Effects of songs with romantic lyrics on compliance with a courtship request." *Psychology of Music* 38(3) (2010).

68  Woollaston, Victoria. "Musicians really are sexier: Scientists find that carrying a guitar increases your chances of getting a date by a third." *DailyMail*, May 7, 2013.

69  Farley, S., et al. "People Will Know We Are in Love: Evidence of Differences Between Vocal Samples Directed Towards Lovers and Friends." *Journal of Nonverbal Behavior* 37(3) (2013): 123.

70  Charles, Dan. "Study Links Warm Hands, Warm Heart." *All Things Considered*. NPR radio. Oct. 25, 2008.

71  Williams, Lawrence, et al. "Experiencing Physical Warmth Promotes Interpersonal Warmth." *Science* 322(5901) (Oct. 24, 2008): 606–7.

72  Ackerman, Joshua, et al. "Incidental Haptic Sensations Influence Social Judgements and Decisions." *Science* 328(5986) (Jun. 25, 2010): 1712–15.

73  Hughes, Susan, et al. "Sex Differences in Romantic Kissing Among College Students: An Evolutionary Perspective." *Evolutionary Psychology* 5(3) (2007): 612–31.

74  Craig, A. D. "How do you feel—now. The anterior insula and human awareness." *Nat Rev Neurosci* 10(1) (Jan 2009): 59.

75  Deen, Ben, et al. "Three Systems of Insular Functional Connectivity Identified with Cluster Analysis." *Cerebral Cortex* 21(7) (Epub Nov. 19, 2010).

76  Chan, Kai Qin, et al. "What do Love and Jealousy Taste Like?" *Emotion* 3(16) (Dec. 2013).

77  Statistic Brain Research Institute. "Online Dating Statistics." (2016) http://www.statisticbrain.com/online-dating-statistics/.

78  Cooper, J. C., et al. "Dorsomedial prefrontal cortex mediates rapid evaluations predicting the outcome of romantic interactions." *Journal of Neuroscience* 32 (Nov. 7, 2012).

79  Sundie, Jill, et al. "Peacocks, Porsches, and Thorstein Veblen: Conspicuous consumption as a sexual signaling system." *Journal of Personality and Social Psychology* 100(4) (Apr. 2001): 664–680.

80  Tracy, Jessica, and Alec Beall. "Happy guys finish last, says new study on sexual attractiveness." *Emotion* 11(6) (2011).

81  Fisher, Helen. "Lust, Attraction, and Attachment in Mammalian Reproduction." *Human Nature* 9(1) (1998): 23–52.

82  Confer, Jaime, et al. "More than just a pretty face: men's priority shifts toward bodily attractiveness in short-term versus long-term mating contexts." *Evolution and Human Behavior* 31(5) (2010): 348.

83  Elliot, A., et al. "Red, Rank and Romance in Women Viewing Men." *Journal of Experimental Psychology: General* 139(3) (2010): 399–417.

84  University of Toronto. "New 'golden ratios' for female facial beauty." *ScienceDaily* (Dec. 17, 2009). www.sciencedaily.com/

releases/2009/12/091216144141.htm. Retrieved September 6, 2013.

85 Blackburn, K., et al. "Emotive hemispheric differences measured in real-life portraits using pupil diameter and subjective aesthetic preferences." *Experimental Brain Research* 219(4) (2012).

86 "Study: 'Love Hormone" Roused by Social Media." Fox News Health online, www.foxnews.com/health/2012/07/12/study-love-hormone-roused-by-social-media/#ixzz2I3mXafFt.

87 Grant, Alexis. "One in Three Female Online Daters Report First-Date Sex." *Houston Chronicle*, August 30, 2007.

88 Association for Psychological Science. "All it takes is a smile (for some guys)." *ScienceDaily* (Dec. 14, 2011). www.sciencedaily.com/releases/2011/12/111213132001.htm. Retrieved June 4, 2013.

89 van der Meij, L., et al. "Men with elevated testosterone levels show more affiliative behaviors during interactions with women." *Proc Biol Sci* 279(1726) (Jan. 7, 2012): 202–208.

90 Fisher, Helen, et al. "Romantic love: A mammalian brain system for mate choice." *Philos Trans R Soc Lond B Biol Sci* 361(1476) (2006): 2173–86.

91 Gingrich, B., et al. "Dopamine D2 receptors in the nucleus accumbens are important for social attachment in female prairie voles (*Microtus ochrogaster*)." *Behavioral Neuroscience* 114 (2000): 173–183.

92 Zhang, Lifen, et al. "Withdrawal from Chronic Nicotine Exposure Alters Dopamine Signaling Dynamics in the Nucleus Accumbens. *Biological Psychiatry* 71(3) (2012).

93 Young, L., et al. "The neurobiology of pair bonding." *Nature Neuroscience* 7(10) (Oct. 2004): 1048–54.

94 Ibid.

95 Ibid.

96 Kringelbach, Morten, and Kent Berridge. "The Functional Neuroanatomy of Pleasure and Happiness." Discovery Medicine NIH Public Access publication, Dec. 22, 2010. http://www.ncbi.nlm.nih.gov/pmc/articles/PMC3008353.

97 Skloot, Rebecca. "How to Change Your Bad Habits." O, The Oprah Magazine, Jan. 2007.

98 Cannon, C., et al. "Is dopamine required for natural reward?" Physiology & Behavior 81(5) (Jul. 2004): 741–8.

99 Fiorino, Dennis, et al. "Dynamic Changes in Nucleus Accumbens Dopamine Efflux During the Coolidge Effect in Male Rats." Journal of Neuroscience 17(12) (Jun. 15, 1997): 4849–55.

100 Young, L., et al. "The neurobiology of pair bonding." Nature Neuroscience 7(10) (Oct. 2004): 1048–54.

101 Ibid.

102 Nagasawa, N., et al. "Dog's gaze at its owner increases owner's urinary oxytocin during social interaction" Hormones and Behavior 55(3) (Mar. 2009): 434–41.

103 Young, L., et al. "The neurobiology of pair bonding." Nature Neuroscience 7(10) (Oct. 2004): 1048–54.

104 Ibid.

105 Ibid.

106 Mohamed Kabbaj, PhD, personal communication, May, 22, 2015.

107 Love, Tiffany. "Oxytocin, motivation and the role of dopamine." Pharmacology Biochemistry and Behavior 119 (Apr. 2014): 49–60.

108 Knut, K., et al. "Reward value of attractiveness and gaze." *Nature* 413 (Oct. 11, 2001).

109 Feldman, R. "Oxytocin and social affiliation in humans" *Hormones and Behavior* 61(3) (Mar. 2012): 380–90.

110 Walum, H., et al. "Variation in the oxytocin receptor gene is associated with pair-bonding and social behavior." *Biological Psychiatry* 71(5) (Mar. 1, 2012): 419–26.

111 Love, Tiffany. "Oxytocin, motivation and the role of dopamine." *Pharmacology Biochemistry and Behavior* 119 (Apr. 2014): 49–60.

112 Schneiderman, Inna, et al. "Oxytocin during initial stages of romantic attachment: Relations to couples' interactive reciprocity." *Psychoneuroendocrinology* 37 (2012): 1277–85.

113 Ibid.

114 Dylewski, Adam. "The Chemistry of Love—Reactions." Video. American Chemical Society (Feb.10, 2014). Retrieved from https://www.youtube.com/watch?v=bp7Ydv5wAPk.

115 Walum, Hasse, et al. "Genetic variation in the vasopressin receptor 1a gene (AVPR1A) associates with pair-bonding behavior in humans." *Proc Natl Acad Sci* 105(37) (Sep. 16, 2008).

116 Wang, H., et al. "Histone deacetylase inhibitors facilitate partner preference formation in female prairie vole." *Nature Neuroscience* 16(7) (Jul. 2011).

117 Lim, M. "Vasopressin-dependent neural circuits underlying pair bond formation in the monogamous prairie vole." *Neuroscience* 125(1) (2004): 35–45.

118 Mazur, A., and A. Booth. "Testosterone and Dominance in Men." *Behavioural and Brain Sciences* 21(3) (Jun. 1998): 353–63.

119 Burnham, T. C., et al. "Men in committed, romantic relationships have lower testosterone." *Hormones and Behavior* 44(2) (Aug. 2003): 119–22.

120 Icahn School of Medicine, Neuroscience Department, Nestler Lab. Brain Reward Pathways. http://neuroscience.mssm.edu/nestler/brainRewardpathways.html.

121 Fisher, Helen, et al. "Romantic love: A mammalian brain system for mate choice." *Philos Trans R Soc Lond B Biol Sci* 361(1476) (2006): 2173–86.

122 The top 20 Traits Women Want in a Man 6/16/15 MSN.com retrieved from http://www.msn.com/en-us/lifestyle/love-sex/the-top-20-traits-women-want-in-a-man.

123 Mobbs, D., et al. "Humor Modulates the Mesolimbic Reward Centers." *Neuron* 40(5) (Dec. 4, 2003): 1041–48.

124 Kosfeld, M., et al. "Oxytocin increases trust in humans." *Nature* 435 (Jun. 2, 2005): 673–76.

125 Kirsch, P., et al. "Oxytocin modulates neural circuitry for social cognition and fear in humans." *Journal of Neuroscience* 25(49) (Dec. 2005): 11489–93.

126 Rosmarin, David, et al. "Incorporating spiritual beliefs into a cognitive model of worry." *Journal of Clinical Psychology* 67(7) (2011).

127 Hölzel, B., et al. "Mindfulness practice leads to increases in regional brain gray matter density." *Psychiatry Research: Neuroimaging* 191(1) (2011): 36.

128 Van Wingen, Guido, et al. "Testosterone reduces amygdala-orbiotfrontal cortex coupling." *Psychoneuroendrocrinology* 33(1) (Jan. 2010).

129 Knight, Emily, et al. "Too Good to Be True: Rhesus Monkeys React Negatively to Better-than-Expected Offers." *PLoS ONE* 8(10) (Oct. 9, 2013).

130 University of Missouri–Columbia (2013, May 14) "Male testosterone levels increase when victorious in competition against rivals, but not friends." *Science Newsline: Psychology.* http://www.sciencenewsline.com/news/2013051415000074.html. Retrieved Sep. 16, 2013.

131 Trumble, Benjamin, et al. "Age-independent increases in male salivary testosterone during horticultural activity among Tsimane forager-farmers." *Evolution and Human Behavior* 34 (2013).

132 University of Missouri–Columbia (2013, May 14) "Male testosterone levels increase when victorious in competition against rivals, but not friends." *Science Newsline: Psychology.* http://www.sciencenewsline.com/news/2013051415000074. html. Retrieved Sep. 16, 2013.

133 Schultz, Wolfram. "Dopamine signals for reward and risk: basic and recent data." *Behavioral and Brain Functions* 6(24) (2010).

134 W. Schultz, personal correspondence, December 3, 2015.

135 American Academy of Neurology. "Dopamine-related Drugs Affect Reward-seeking Behavior." *ScienceDaily* (Apr. 30, 2007). www.sciencedaily.com/releases/2007/04/070427072318.htm. Retrieved July 12, 2013.

136 Zeki, S. "The Neurobiology of Love." *FEBS Letters* 581 (2007): 2575–79.

137 Fisher, Helen, et al. "Romantic love: A mammalian brain system for mate choice." *Philos Trans R Soc Lond B Biol Sci* 361(1476) (2006): 2173–86.

138   Phelan, Jay. *What is Life? A Guide to Biology*. New York: W. H. Freeman, 2010: 355.

139   Ibid.

140   Liza, A., et al. "Perception of male-male competition influences *Drosophila* copulation behavior even in species where females rarely remate." *Biology Letters* (2011).

141   Brehrendt, Greg, and Liz Tuccillo. *He's Just Not That Into You: The No-Excuse Truth to Understanding Guys*. New York: Simon Spotlight Entertainment, 2004.

142   Ibid.

143   Clark, Russell, et al. "Gender Differences in Receptivity to Sexual Offers." *Journal of Psychology & Human Sexuality* 2(1) (1989).

144   Zeki, S. "The Neurobiology of Love." *FEBS Letters* 581 (2007): 2575–79.

145   Russell, Steve. "Online dating relationship ends badly, $1.3M later." *The Star*, Jul. 11, 2014.

146   Wyart, C., et al. "Smelling a single component of male sweat alters levels of cortisol in women." *J. Neurosci* 27(6) (Feb. 7, 2007): 1261–5.

147   Tom, S., et al. "The Neural Basis of Loss Aversion in Decision-Making Under Risk." *Science* 315 (Jan. 26, 2007).

148   Sage Publications. "Friendship, Timing Key Differences Between US, Eastern European Love." *ScienceDaily*, Aug. 17, 2011. (Summary of de Munck, V. C., et al., *Cross-Cultural Research* 45(2), 2011.)

149   Wang, H., et al. "Histone deacetylase inhibitors facilitate partner preference formation in female prairie vole." *Nature Neuroscience* 16(7) (Jul. 2011).

150  Severo, Richard. "William Proxmire, Maverick Democratic Senator From Wisconsin, Is Dead at 90." *New York Times*, Dec. 16, 2005.

151  Zeki, S. "The Neurobiology of Love." *FEBS Letters* 581 (2007): 2575–79.

152  Bartels, Andreas, et al. "The neural correlates of maternal and romantic love." *NeuroImage* 21 (2004): 1155–66.

153  Zeki, S. "The Neurobiology of Love." *FEBS Letters* 581 (2007): 2575–79.

154  Loyola University Healthy System. "What falling in love does to your heart and brain." *ScienceDaily*, Feb. 6, 2014.

155  Bartels, Andreas, et al. "The neural correlates of maternal and romantic love." *NeuroImage* 21 (2004): 1155–66.

156  Zeki, S. "The Neurobiology of Love." *FEBS Letters* 581 (2007): 2575–79.

157  Xiaomeng, X., et al. "Regional brain activity during early-stage intense romantic love predicted relationship outcomes after 40 months: An fMRI assessment." *Neuroscience Letters* 526 (2012): 33–38.

158  Lynch, Dennis. "Valentine's Day Jailbreak: Joseph Andrew Dekenipp Escaped Jail to Meet His Girlfriend at Saloon." *International Business Times* Feb. 19, 2014. http://www.ibtimes. com/valentines-day-jailbreak-joseph-andrew-dekenipp-es-caped-jail-meet-his-girlfriend-saloon-1555826.

159  D'Argembeau, Arnaud. "On the Role of the Ventromedial Prefrontal Cortex in Self-Processing: The Valuation Hypothesis." *Frontier of Human Neuroscience* 7 (2013): 372.

160  Zeki, S. "The Neurobiology of Love." *FEBS Letters* 581 (2007): 2575–79.

161 Van Steenbergen, Henk, et al. "Reduced cognitive control in passionate lovers." *Motivation and Emotion* 38(3) (2014).

162 Zeki, S. "The Neurobiology of Love." *FEBS Letters* 581 (2007): 2575–79.

163 Bartels, Andreas, et al. "The neural basis of romantic love." *NeuroReport* 11(27) (Nov. 2000).

164 McIntyre, Matthew, et al. "Romantic involvement often reduces men's testosterone levels—but not always: the moderating role of extrapair sexual interest." *Journal of Personality and Social Psychology* 91(4) (2006): 642–51.

165 Ananthaswamy, Anil. "Love, the great gender bender." *New Scientist*, May 8, 2004.

166 Law, Bridget Murray. "Hormones & desire: Hormones associated with the menstrual cycle appear to drive sexual attraction more than we know." *American Psychological Association* 42(3) (Mar. 2011).

167 Gray, Peter, et al. "Human Male Pair Bonding and Testosterone." *Human Nature* 15(2) (Jun. 2004): 119–31.

168 Panzica, G. C. "The sexually dimorphic medial preoptic nucleus of quail: A key brain area mediating steroid action on male sexual behavior." *Front Neuroendocrinol* 17(1) (Jan. 1996): 51–125.

169 Baskerville, T., and A. Douglas. "Dopamine and Oxytocin Interactions Underlying Behaviors: Potential on Contributions to Behavioral Disorders." *CNS Neuroscience & Therapeutics* 16(3) (2010).

170 Schneiderman, Inna, et al. "Oxytocin during initial stages of romantic attachment: Relations to couples' interactive reciprocity." *Psychoneuroendocrinology* 37 (2012): 1277–85.

171   Ibid.

172   Gravotta, Luciana. "Be Mine Forever: Oxytocin May Help Build Long-Lasting Love." *Scientific American,* Feb. 12, 2013.

173   Ibid.

174   "The 'love hormone' oxytocin may keep men faithful in relationships." *NY Daily News,* Nov. 15, 2012.

175   Scheele, Dirk, et al. "Oxytocin enhances brain reward system responses in men viewing the face of their female partner." *Proc Natl Acad Sci* 110(50) (2013).

176   Neumann, Inga. "Oxytocin: The Neuropeptide of Love Reveals Some of Its Secrets." *Cell Metabolism* 5(4) (Apr. 2007).

177   Marazziti, Donatella, et al. "Hormonal changes when falling in love." *Psychoneuroendocrinology* 29(7) (Aug. 2004): 931–36.

178   Ibid.

179   Zeki, S. "The Neurobiology of Love." *FEBS Letters* 581 (2007): 2575–79.

180   Meloy, J. Reid, et al. "Some Thoughts on the Neurobiology of Stalking." *Journal of Forensic Science* 50(6) (Nov. 2005).

181   Zeki, S. "The Neurobiology of Love." *FEBS Letters* 581 (2007): 2575–79.

182   Fisher, Helen. "Lust, Attraction, and Attachment in Mammalian Reproduction." *Human Nature* 9(1) (1998): 23–52.

183   Loving, Timothy, et al. "Passionate love and relationship thinkers: Experimental evidence for acute cortisol elevations in women." *Psychoneuroendocrinology* 34(6) (2009): 939–46.

184   Ibid.

185   Kirschbaum, C., et al. "Impact of gender, menstrual cycle phase, and oral contraceptives on the activity of the

hypothalamus-pituitary-adrenal axis." *Psychosomatic Medicine* 61(2) (Mar.-Apr. 1999): 154–62.

186  Younger, Jarred, et al. "Viewing Pictures of a Romantic Partner Reduces Experimental Pain: Involvement of Neural Reward Systems." *PLoS ONE* (Oct. 13, 2010).

187  Ibid.

188  Koneru, Amupama, et al. "Endogenous Opioids: Their Physiological Role and Receptors." *Global Journal of Pharmacology* 3(3) (2009): 149–53.

189  Bayliss, Kelly. "Couple Caught Having Sex on Chipotle Roof: Police." NBC10.com. http://www.nbcphiladelphia.com/news/local/Couple-Arrested-for-Having-Sex-on-Chipotle-Roof-267032481.html.

190  Koneru, Amupama, et al. "Endogenous Opioids: Their Physiological Role and Receptors." *Global Journal of Pharmacology* 3(3) (2009): 149–53.

191  Emanuele, Enzo, et al. "Raised plasma nerve growth factor levels associated with early-stage romantic love." *Psychoneuroendocrinology* 31(3) (2006): 288–94.

192  Ibid.

193  Marazziti, D., et al. "Research Letter: Brain-derived neurotropic factor in romantic attachment." *Psychological Medicine* 39 (2009): 1927–30.

194  Ibid.

195  Vargas-Perez, Hector, et al. "Ventral Tegmental Area BDNF Induces an Opiate-Dependent-Like Reward State in Naïve Rats." *Science* 324(5935) (Jun. 26, 1009): 1732–34.

196  Aron, Arthur, et al. "Falling in Love: Prospective Studies

of Self-Concept Change." *Journal of Personality and Social Psychology* 69(6) (1995): 1102–12.

197  Koneru, Amupama, et al. "Endogenous Opioids: Their Physiological Role and Receptors." *Global Journal of Pharmacology* 3(3) (2009): 149–53.

198  Zeki, S. "The Neurobiology of Love." *FEBS Letters* 581 (2007): 2575–79.

199  Marazziti, Donatella, and Stefano Baroni. "Romantic love: the mystery of its biological roots." *Clinical Neuropsychiatry* 9(1) (Feb.-Mar. 2012).

200  de Boer, A., et al. "Love is more than just a kiss: A neurobiological perspective on love and affection." *Neuroscience* 201 (2012): 114–24.

201  Marazziti, Donatella, et al. "Hormonal changes when falling in love." *Psychoneuroendocrinology* 29(7) (Aug. 2004): 931–36.

202  Ibid.

203  Acevedo, B., et al. "Neural correlates of long-term intense romantic love." *Social Cognitive and Affective Neuroscience* 7(2) (Feb. 2012): 149–59.

204  Fisher, H. E. "The Nature of Romantic Love." *Journal of NIH Research* 6(4) (1994): 59–64.

205  Bartels, Andreas, et al. "The neural basis of romantic love." *NeuroReport* 11(27) (Nov. 2000).

206  Ramachandran, V. S. *The Tell-Tale Brain: A Neuroscientist's Quest for What Makes Us Human.* New York: W. W. Norton, 2011.

207  Acevedo, B., et al. "Neural correlates of long-term intense romantic love." *Social Cognitive and Affective Neuroscience* 7(2) (Feb. 2012): 149–59.

208 Ibid.

209 Beauregard, M., et al. "The neural basis of unconditional love." *Psychiatry Research: Neuroimaging* 172(2) (May 15, 2009): 93–98.

210 Moll, J., et al. "The Neural Correlates of Moral Sensitivity: A Functional Magnetic Resonance Imaging Investigation of Basic and Moral Emotions." *Journal of Neuroscience* 22(7) (Apr. 1, 2002): 2730–36.

211 Takahashi, Hidehiko, et al. "Neural Correlates of Human Virtue Judgment." *Cerebral Cortex* 18(8) (Aug. 2008): 1886–91.

212 Engstrom, M., et al. "Brain Activation During Compassion Meditation: A Case Study." *Journal of Alternative and Complementary Medicine* 16(5) (May 2010): 597–99.

213 Gonzaga, Gian, et al. "Love, desire, and the suppression of thoughts of romantic alternatives." *Evolution and Human Behavior* 29 (2008): 119–26.

214 Pronk, T., et al. "How can you resist? Executive control helps romantically involved individuals to stay faithful." *Journal of Personality and Social Psychology* 100(5) (May 2011): 827–37.

215 Matsunaga, M., et al. "Genetic variations in the serotonin transporter gene-linked polymorphic region influence attraction for a favorite person and the associated interactions between the central nervous and immune system. *Neuroscience Letters* 468 (2010): 211–15.

216 Kiecolt-Glaser, J., et al. "Marriage and Health: His and Hers." *Psychological Bulletin* 127(4) (2001): 472–503.

217 Fair, V., et al. "Epigenetic inheritance of a cocaine-resistance phenotype." *Nature Neuroscience* 16 (2012).

218 Finn, C., et al. "Recent Decreases in Specific Interpretation

Biases Predict Decreases in Neuroticism: Evidence From a Longitudinal Study With Young Adult Couples." *Personality* 83(3) (2014).

219  Acevedo, B., et al. "Neural correlates of long-term intense romantic love." *Social Cognitive and Affective Neuroscience* 7(2) (Feb. 2012): 149–59.

220  Ibid.

221  Acevedo, B., and A. Aron. "Does a Long-Term Relationship Kill Romantic Love?" *Review of General Psychology* 13(1) (2009): 59–65.

222  Aron, A., et al. "The experimental generation of interpersonal closeness: a procedure and some preliminary findings." *Personality & Social Psychology Bulletin* 23(4) (April 1997): 363.

223  Epstude, Kai, et al. "Seeing love, or seeing lust: How people interpret ambiguous romantic situations." *Journal of Experimental Social Psychology* 47 (2011): 1017–20.

224  Marazziti, D., et al. "Research Letter: Brain-derived neurotropic factor in romantic attachment." *Psychological Medicine* 39 (2009): 1927–30.

225  Boderman, G., et al. "The role of stress in divorce: A three-nation retrospective study." *Journal of Social and Personal Relationships* 24(5) (Oct. 2007): 707–28.

226  Davidson, R., et al. "Social influences on neuroplasticity: stress and interventions to promote well-being." *Nature Neuroscience* 15 (2012): 689–95.

227  Ibid.

228  Ibid.

229  Arnsten, A., et al. "This is Your Brain in Meltdown." *Scientific American* 306(4) (Apr. 2012): 48–53.

230  Lisitsa, Ellie. "The Four Horsemen: The Antidotes." Gottman Relationship Blog, The Gottman Institute. https://www.gottman.com/blog/the-four-horsemen-the-antidotes/.

231  Xu, X., et al. "Reward and Motivation Systems: A Brain Mapping Study of Early-Stage Intense Romantic Love in Chinese Participants." *Human Brain Mapping* 32 (2011): 249–57.

232  Gaia, V. "Watching the brain 'switch off' self-awareness." *The New Scientist*, Apr. 19, 2006.

233  Vaillant, G. "Positive Emotions, Spirituality and the Practice of Psychiatry." *Mental Health, Spirituality, Mind* 6(1) (2008): 48–62.

234  Ibid.

235  Wolchover, Natalie. "Brain Scans Could reveal If Your Relationship Will Last." *LiveScience*, February 14, 2012. http://www.livescience.com/18468-relationship-longevity-brain-scans.html.

236  Ramachandran, V. S. *The Tell-Tale Brain: A Neuroscientist's Quest for What Makes Us Human.* New York: W. W. Norton, 2011.

237  Fisher, H. "Lasting Love: The Secret To Long-Term Relationships." *Huffington Post*, July 8, 2013.

238  O'Leary, K. D., et al. "Is Long-Term Love More Than A Rare Phenomenon? If So, What Are Its Correlates?" *Social Psychological and Personality Science* 3(2) (Mar. 2012): 241–249.

239  Holmes, J., et al. "A leap of faith? Positive illusions in romantic relationships." *Personality & Social Psychology Bulletin.* 23(6) (June 1997): 586.

240  Ibid.

241  Ibid.

242  Ibid.

243  Ibid.

244  Gigy, Lynn, et al. "Reasons for Divorce: Perspectives of Divorcing Men and Women." *Journal of Divorce & Remarriage* 18(1–2), 1993.

245  Acevedo, B., et al. "Neural correlates of long-term intense romantic love." *Social Cognitive and Affective Neuroscience* 7(2) (Feb. 2012): 149–59.

246  Ibid.

247  Aron, A., et al. "Couple's Shared Participation in Novel and Arousing Activities and Experienced Relationship Quality." *Journal of Personality and Social Psychology* 78(2) (2000): 273–84.

248  Welker, K., et al. "Effects of self-disclosure and responsiveness between couples on passionate love within couples." *Personal Relationships* 21 (2014): 692–708.

249  Ortigue, S., et al. "The neural basis of love as subliminal prime: An event-related fMRI study." *Journal of Cognitive Neuroscience* 19(7) (Jul. 2007): 1218–30.

250  Aron, A. "Marital Satisfaction and Passionate Love." *Journal of Social and Personal Relationships* 12(1) (Feb. 1995): 139–46.

251  Mazur, A., and A. Booth. "Testosterone and Dominance in Men." *Behavioural and Brain Sciences* 21(3) (Jun. 1998): 353–63.

252  Ibid.

253  Vongas, J., et al. "Competing Sexes, Power, and Testosterone: How Winning and Losing Affect People's Empathic Responses and What this Means for Organizations." *Applied Psychology: An International Review* 64(2) (2015): 308–37.

254  Algoe, S., et al. "It's the Little Things: Everyday Gratitude as a Booster Shot for Romantic Relationships." *Personal Relationships* 17 (2010): 217–33.

255 Takahashi, Hidehiko, et al. "Neural Correlates of Human Virtue Judgment." *Cerebral Cortex* 18(8) (Aug. 2008): 1886–91.

256 Guerra, P., et al. "Viewing Loved Faces Inhibits Defense Reactions: A Health-Promotion Mechanism?" *PLoS ONE* 7(7) (2012).

257 Ibid.

258 Baumgarter, T., et al. "Oxytocin Shapes Neural Circuitry to Trust and Trust Adaptations in Humans." *Neuron* 58 (May 22, 2008): 639–50.

259 Hiller, J. "Gender differences in sexual motivation." *Journal of Men's Health & Gender* 2(3) (Sep. 2005): 339.

260 Holmes, J., et al. "A leap of faith? Positive illusions in romantic relationships." *Personality & Social Psychology Bulletin*. 23(6) (June 1997): 586.

261 Esch, T., et al. "The Neurobiology of Love." *Neuroendrocrinology Letters* 26(3) (2005): 175–92.

262 Felix, N., et al. "Satisfaction with Love Life Across the Adult Life Span." *Applied Research in Quality of Life* 10(2) (Jun. 2015).

263 Frassica, M. "What is Love? U of L professors apply some hard science to a 'touchy-feely topic.'" *The Courier-Journal*, Feb. 9, 2014.